Don't Marry an American

Don't Marry an American

a memoir of coming to America

*Finding Love, a Better Life
and Two Countries to Call Home*

Ben Kyriagis

EPIDEXION BOOKS

MINNEAPOLIS, MINNESOTA

Published by: EPIDEXION BOOKS - Minneapolis, Minnesota
www.Epidexionbooks.com

Print ISBN No: 978-1-7371246-0-3
eBook ISBN No: 978-1-7371246-1-0

Book Design by: MAYFLY DESIGN - Minneapolis, Minnesota.

Cover photo: By Ben Kyriagis
View from above the village of Krania, on Mount Olympus Greece, toward the
Aegean Sea and Mount Kissavos.

Author's photo by: Vania Tloupa of Tloupas Photography. Daughter of photographer
Takis Tloupas. July 2021 in the city of Larissa, Greece.

FIRST EDITION
Printed in the United States of America, on FSC and SFI Certified paper, from
sustainably harvested forests.

CONTENTS

*Everything is held together with stories. That is all
that is holding us together, stories and compassion.*

BARRY LOPEZ

* ONE *

What if the American Is Shelley?

CONSIDER TWO RAINDROPS that fall together on the side of a mountain. Sliding downhill, they blend with other drops, gradually picking up speed to form a rivulet that runs into a creek. The creek empties into a river, and soon the raindrops are bobbing in a river wave, moving faster and faster, and sometimes they slow down to a lazy, leisurely flow.

In boredom and excitement, the drops move through valleys, villages, and cities. Along the way, they change in color and content. Finally, they slide home in the undertow of a friendly sea wave, into the broad arms of an ocean bay. There they rest for a while, loitering among their salty neighbors. Later, after they're heated by the sun, the drops evaporate and rise again to join a rain cloud and start a new life cycle, perhaps on another mountain, into a new river, and onward to the ocean.

Imagine for a moment that the raindrops, while in the clouds, were able to contemplate their life cycles, starting from the time they fell on the mountainsides, through their adventuresome journeys to the ocean and up into the clouds. What stories they would tell!

At times we may feel that our lives are as insignificant as the lives of the raindrops. But we can survey our lives and learn where we came from, the choices we have made, what we have learned along the way, and share our stories.

As two raindrops help form the essence of an enormous ocean, our own, individual stories, when shared, contribute to the essence of the story of humanity, on its magnificent journey through history.

In the fall of 1975, I was starting my second year at the University of Wisconsin at Eau Claire, a university known for its beautiful campus and its schools of business, education, and nursing. The total enrollment was around ten thousand, including two hundred international students. I was among this small group and the only student from Greece. I'll get to how I ended up at Eau Claire later.

I was excited about the beginning of the new semester and looked forward to learning new things and meeting new classmates, especially beautiful women. Because I had worked for two years after graduating high school, I was older than the other students in my class. I had thick dark hair that I cut only once a year to save money, and a full beard. I was not what anyone would call a handsome man but let's just say I had an interesting face. I hoped that my long hair and beard projected maturity and sophistication, even though, in my first year at the university, my success with women had been less than great.

On Tuesday, September 2, 1975, a cool and gray fall morning, and the first day of the semester, I walked into Room 317, on the third floor of Schneider Hall. I was in my usual jeans and tennis shoes, with a light bomber jacket over my short-sleeved shirt. My advanced economics class met at eight a.m., and as usual for my early morning classes, I arrived a few minutes late, and the teacher had already started his introduction. I sat as quietly as I could in the back of the room, close to the door, laid my backpack down, and took off my jacket.

The classroom was one of the smallest I had seen on campus and had gray painted walls. About a dozen guys and a couple of girls were in front of me and a few empty chairs. The chairs were small and old-fashioned, the type with a tiny desk space attached to the arm.

The two small windows on the right did not allow in enough light and the ceiling lights were on. The morning drab mood of the classroom matched the gray sky outside. The only other features of the

DON'T MARRY AN AMERICAN

room were a whiteboard and a small desk for the professor, who stood in front of it as he spoke.

The professor was a native of India with a strong, difficult-to-understand accent. I was self-conscious about my own accent, and I hoped that it was not as strong. As the professor was going through the class syllabus, a student in front and to the right of me turned around in his chair and motioned for me to take the extra syllabus handouts he was holding in his hand. I quickly got up, grabbed them, and returned to my chair. There were three or four sets of the two-page handout.

After ten minutes of going over the syllabus and the class requirements, I got the impression that this class was not going to be among my favorites that semester.

It was about eight fifteen when the door suddenly opened and in walked an attractive young woman, red in the face, probably from running, and maybe from the embarrassment of being late. She slid quietly into the chair to my left. For a moment, it seemed like no one else had noticed her slip into the room.

As I was checking out my new neighbor, somewhat discreetly, the beautiful newcomer turned to me with a most genuine, sweet, and radiant smile. Suddenly, the classroom became brighter and filled with color. I was mentally transported to a beautiful, green meadow full of wildflowers and bird songs. Captivated by the face with the sweet smile and blue eyes, I grinned with pleasure and said, right out loud, "Hiii!"

That *Hiii!* was full of nothing but admiration and eagerness and it caused the turning of all the heads in the class in our direction. The beauty smiled nervously, blushed, and lowered her head. I quickly turned my head toward the window on my right, trying to hide that I was the originator of that loud, enthusiastic greeting. I waited a few moments for everyone's attention to return to the teacher and then I handed my neighbor one of the copies of the class syllabus. She took it with a smile and with her perfect teeth mouthed "Thank you." I smiled back and reluctantly turned my gaze back to the professor.

I tried but could not pay enough attention to his words. Instead, I was studying, as inconspicuously as I could, the beautiful classmate to my left. She had luxurious, lightly curled blond/brown hair parted in the middle and touching her shoulders. Under a light blue jacket, which she'd kept on, I could see parts of a red and white gingham shirt. Blue jeans and tennis shoes completed her outfit. She was perhaps a couple of inches shorter than my five feet ten.

I was also trying to figure out what had just happened. What had caused me to say hi with such enthusiasm, without thinking? It had to be her pretty face with full lips, clear blue eyes, and a genuine smile.

I think that early in life we get crazy ideas about certain things. I always knew that I would marry a blond, blue-eyed girl. Is this knowledge in our genes?

If so, how do the genes know? And how do they get that information to our brains?

Blue eyes and blond hair were uncommon in the Greek village I grew up in. I hadn't seen many blond, blue-eyed girls in my youth. Perhaps my subconscious equated the rarity of these features with desirability. The charming classmate to my left must have touched that nerve in my subconscious.

Marriage was the last thing on my mind. I was not looking for a wife, far from it. I was determined that I would not get married until I was thirty. Greece was my home. I was only a visitor to America. My clear and definite plan was to return to Greece right after graduation. I was so sure about this plan that before I left Greece to study in America, I made a promise to my parents that I would not marry an American, and after I received my diploma, I would return to Greece.

What I wanted was a girlfriend, but even though I didn't need to be overly selective, I had always been a sucker for beauty. That girl with the megaton smile, sitting to my left in that small classroom, had stirred in me an attraction and excitement I had never felt before.

At some point, I realized that the class was going to be over soon, and I had to do something. *What if Miss Beautiful doesn't like the class and drops it and I never see her again? What if I decide to drop the class? Well, I can't do that. I am an economics major, and this is a required class.*

After a while, I came up with a simple plan: as soon as the class bell rang, I would follow her and ask for her phone number, right then and there. I had never done this before, and I told myself—or perhaps it was my genes telling me—*You must act, Ben. This attractive girl smiled at you with the warmth of a Greek summer day.*

Then the bell rang! The blue eyes smiled at me and her mouth followed, quicker this time, and before I had a chance to smile back or say anything, she stood up and was gone.

I grabbed my class papers and threw them in my backpack, put on my jacket, stuck a pen and piece of paper in my right pocket, and got out of that classroom as fast as I could. I scanned the hallway, which was full of students rushing about, but I saw no sign of Miss Beautiful. I walked as fast as I could through the crowded hallway to the busy stairway and went down as fast as the traffic allowed to the ground floor lobby. There, about five steps ahead of me, among a crowd of students, I saw the back of her golden hair. She had slowed down because the student traffic had formed a slow-moving bottleneck through the glass doors leading outside.

That gave me time to navigate the traffic, position myself behind her, and touch her left shoulder. We were standing in the lobby surrounded by students walking slowly past us in both directions, talking with their friends and classmates.

She turned to me and smiled. I was standing in front of her, catching my breath from running down the stairs as I looked into her eyes.

"Gee!" I said, smiling, "you left so fast! I didn't get a chance to talk to you."

"I have another class in the upper campus in ten minutes and I don't want to be late for that one too!" she said.

"What is your name?" I asked, hoping she wouldn't notice my accent, fearing it might be a turnoff.

"Shelley," she answered, smiling.

"Selly?" I said, as I had never heard that name before and had a hard time pronouncing the *sh* sound.

"Shelley!" she repeated.

"Shelley!" I got it this time. "That's not a common name! I would really like to get to know you better, Shelley, so if you give me your phone number, I will call you and we can meet sometime soon!"

"Sure!" she said with a slight grin on her lips. I handed her my pen and paper. She placed the paper on her left palm and wrote the number. When she finished, she looked at me and asked, "Where are you from?"

Oh, shit! She noticed my accent, I thought, but instead of answering, I said, "Can you guess?"

Shelley looked impatient. She handed me the paper and pen, and after I saw there was a phone number, I slid them in my pocket as she started walking toward the glass doors.

I followed her saying "Just guess a country."

As we walked through the doors, Shelley said, "Gee, I don't know, Mexico?" and kept walking.

I wasn't able to keep up with her as students were crowding me on both sides. After a few steps I managed to reach her side and said, "Mexico?" with a questioning and surprising tone in my voice. I considered Mexico to be beneath me, as I have always been a proud Greek.

"Nah! I'm from Greece!" I exclaimed, and added quickly, "I will call you this evening, Shelley." Then I turned right, toward the building of my next class.

We were now well outside of Schneider Hall, where the student traffic was thinner. I took a few steps and then heard Shelley say, "Hey! Wait a minute!"

I turned and walked back to her, quickly, smiling. As I approached, she said, "You didn't even tell me your name!" in a tone of mild accusation that made me feel guilty.

"Oh! Sorry about that. My Greek name is Evangelos, but everyone calls me Ben."

"I think I can remember Ben. Can I call you Ben?"

"Of course, I've had that nickname for a long time."

"I have to go to my next class now, Ben, so I'll see you later or in the next class."

"Yes!" I said, smiling. "I'll call you this evening."

Shelley turned around to walk in the direction of the upper campus. She walked quickly, in a confident manner, and held her head high. She looked taller than most students around her. I exhaled a sigh of relief and satisfaction. The sigh was probably from my genes. The satisfaction was all mine. As I walked to my next class, I found it hard to erase the grin off my face.

This first encounter with Shelley lasted only a few minutes. But it left such an impression on my mind that I can still relive it now as if it happened yesterday and not forty-five years ago. I had never had the impulse to follow a girl after class to get her phone number. Sometimes I wonder what would have happened if I had not run after Shelley on that first day of class. But I'm glad I did.

I didn't know if I was experiencing love at first sight or plain lust. I knew it was something different than I had felt before. I was fascinated with the girl with the beautiful blue eyes and the sweet smile. I knew that I wanted to get to know her better, and very soon.

Later that day I called Shelley, and we made plans to meet at the Student Union cafeteria the following day.

We seemed comfortable with each other as we looked into each other's eyes. I with admiration for Shelley's attractive face and cheerful disposition, and Shelley with seeming curiosity about this foreign student who was so forward and so obviously interested in her. Our conversation flowed as if we had known each other for a long time.

Shelley was a small-town girl. She had started college as a music major—piano and voice—and later changed to business management. She loved music but did not like to perform in front of an audience. We were both twenty-one. Other than that, and the economics class, we didn't have much in common. She was a listener, and I a talker. But she had her own views about life. As the oldest of five, she had pushed the boundaries of her parents' discipline and developed a strong, independent spirit.

Soon after that first date, we started spending our time between classes and some evenings together, doing some studying, but mostly getting to know each other. In late September and early October of that year, we spent many hours together sitting on the grass under golden maple trees, enjoying the glory of the fall colors, talking about our economics class and about life. We also enjoyed going to the movies and listening to music—jazz, folk, Bob Dylan, Paul Simon, James Taylor, and others.

Shelley showed great interest in my stories about life in Greece and my interest in history, politics, and philosophy. I enjoyed her beauty, her company, and even her frequent challenges to my highfalutin theories and ideas. She wasn't an intellectual type, but she had developed a finely tuned B.S. detector and was not bashful about using it. We were becoming a couple with an easy, natural, and comfortable attachment.

We had different backgrounds. Shelley was the oldest daughter of a second-generation, middle-class dentist, with mostly Scandinavian heritage. I was the second son of a lower-class Greek construction worker. I was able to attend the university because of a scholarship. Shelley's parents and both sets of her grandparents were college-educated. My parents had a sixth-grade education, and I was the first person on both sides of my family to attend university. But we felt that we had compatible personalities and enjoyed being together.

From my early days with Shelley, I loved her smell. She didn't wear perfume. It was her natural scent that invaded my senses when I kissed her hands, her lips, or when we were simply close to each other. The best way I can describe it is a combination of the warm homemade bread my mother baked when I was a child and the intense, deep aroma of heirloom roses. Just being with her, touching her, was a feast for all my senses. Shelley often told me that she liked my smell. Maybe this is part of what couples have in mind when they talk about having good chemistry.

One of my first presents to Shelley was the book *Zorba the Greek* by Nikos Kazantzakis. I wanted to expose her to Greek culture and the philosophy of Zorba, the main hero of the book, in the hope that she would understand and appreciate my Greek background.

Even though I was an economics major, I had talked to Shelley about my interest in philosophy and my search for my philosophy of life. I had read several of Kazantzakis's books, in Greece, and was impressed with his lifelong search for understanding and enlightenment. His philosophy was based on what the French philosopher Henri Bergson called the *élan vital*, the creative force we can cultivate and use to achieve what we want in life.

I told Shelley that my top priority was to develop my own philosophy to create the best life I could, because being so far away from my family and my country, I could only depend on myself. It is obvious to me now that this was a selfish and limited point of view, something Shelley understood right away. She would smile or laugh at my rather unusual and grandiose views of my place in the world and the universe. She found them entertaining, easy to ignore, and she told me so. That did not bother me. I found her reaction instructive as it forced me to reexamine my assumptions. I liked her confidence and strength.

The semester went by fast. We struggled with our economics class and were relieved when it was over. We both earned Cs, and the realization that economics would be better off without us, and vice versa. Shelley stayed with her business administration-management major, and I switched to business administration-marketing, but we continued to be a couple.

In 1975, for Christmas break, I suggested, and Shelley agreed, that we would take a cross-country road trip together, in her car, all the way to California. We had saved some money for the trip and were going to take two weeks to visit my Greek friends attending universities in Colorado and California. To share the cost of gasoline and some driving time, we took a couple of riders as far as Colorado.

On a cold winter day a few days before Christmas, we set out in Shelley's old Chevy Nova. Farzad, a male Iranian student, and a female student whose name I do not recall, rode with us. After driving straight through to Denver, we dropped off our riders there. Then we drove to Boulder, where the University of Colorado is located. We stayed in Boulder three nights, just the two of us, in the apartment of a Greek friend who was out of town.

This was Shelley's first Christmas away from her family. Her parents were not pleased when she told them a month earlier that over the Christmas holidays she was driving with Ben, her Greek boyfriend, whom they had not yet met, to California and back. They had tried to change her mind but could not. Shelley told them that, as a twenty-one-year-old adult, she could make her own decisions. I wasn't surprised because I had seen her strong, independent personality in the brief time I'd known her. But it is usually harder for parents of daughters to accept their independence, even at twenty-one.

On Christmas Eve, in downtown Boulder, we watched the movie *Mahogany*, with Diana Ross and Billy Dee Williams. It was a romantic drama with a powerful message delivered by Williams at the end of the film: "Success is nothing without someone you love to share it with." Even though this was an indirect denunciation of my philosophy of building a successful life depending only on oneself, Shelley and I found the message timely and befitting our young and blossoming relationship. Afterward we had a lively conversation about the movie, and Shelley was pleased that I agreed with its main idea. She had started to change me.

The next day, Christmas, it was snowing. We had gone grocery shopping the previous day and had planned to spend the day in the apartment. For dinner I cooked a chicken with oregano and lemon potatoes in the oven, one of my favorite Greek recipes, and we shared a bottle of wine. This was our first Christmas together.

In the afternoon, we called Shelley's parents in Amery, Wisconsin, and my parents in Larissa, Greece. Shelley's parents were relieved that their daughter was safe. My parents were pleased to hear from me on Christmas as I could not afford to call them often. They weren't worried about me getting married and neither was I. Shelley, and I were pleased to be together in a nice, cozy apartment with television and music, and to be getting along so well, considering we'd met only four short months earlier.

On the second day of Christmas, we were invited to a party in Denver with about half a dozen Greek university students, most of them friends from my hometown, Larissa. The tasty Greek appetizers and Greek wine and music on the stereo were followed by spontaneous Greek dancing. All of us were missing our families, and the music transported us to Greece.

This was the first time that Shelley had been exposed to a group of Greeks and the exuberance of a Greek celebration. Before I had a chance to worry about how she would react, she jumped right in. Shelley loved dancing. Without any prior Greek dancing experience, she was learning the different dances, impressing all the Greeks with her attitude.

Everyone there spoke English, so language was not a problem. Shelley charmed them all with her pleasant, unassuming personality, her easy smile and friendliness. She fit in effortlessly. Some of my Greek friends seemed jealous of me because of my girlfriend. Before this party, I had felt fortunate to be dating Shelley. Now I felt even luckier. Shelley's total delight in and acceptance of this slice of Greek culture reinforced my appreciation of her talents and personality.

The next day we left Colorado for Southern California, arriving two days later. We spent New Year's Eve with Greek friends in a suburb of Los Angeles. We enjoyed the mild California weather, and a daytrip to San Diego. Other than that, California did not impress me.

The drive back from Los Angeles to Denver, however, will stay with me for the rest of my life. We took the northern route, Interstate 70, which goes through Utah and takes about sixteen hours to reach Denver.

We left early in the morning, counting on good forecasts for California and Colorado. These were the days before GPS. We had a map in the car, but it was not detailed. By mid-afternoon we were somewhere in Utah when suddenly the weather changed. Thick clouds moved in fast and soon it started to snow. At first the snow was light but before long it was coming down thick and fast. There was hardly any traffic in front of us, behind us, or in the opposite direction.

We were in the middle of nowhere, in the center of the worst snowstorm that either of us had experienced. We took a quick inventory. We had enough gas for about an hour. The snow was piling up fast on the road and the car was struggling through it. The windshield wipers were frantic, at the highest speed, but the visibility was barely enough to see a few feet in front of the car. We knew that if we ended up in a ditch or the car was disabled, we would have to spend the night in the car. We were not prepared for that.

From our map, we could not figure exactly where we were. We knew we had to get off the road at the first town we came to and find a hotel to spend the night. But we had no idea how far away that might be.

I kept driving anxiously, keeping my eyes glued to the windshield, peering at the road, and wishing for that exit sign. Time slowed down to a crawl. Eventually we lost track of how long we had been driving in this whiteout. Perhaps it was only half an hour, but it seemed like hours. We were worried we would either run out of gas or slide off the road, and either way we would be in real danger.

Finally, we saw the sign for an exit with the name of a town. We had never heard of the place and I've forgotten its name, but we were never more excited about an exit in our lives. We slowed down some but not too much—we were afraid of getting stuck. Fortunately, we did not miss the exit, and within ten to fifteen minutes, we were downtown checking in at the only hotel in town, for the last room they had available. The hotel clerk told us that the snowstorm had brought them a lot of travelers they had not expected.

What a relief to finally be safe in a warm place! The snow was still coming down and it continued through most of the night. We decided to have a nice dinner at the restaurant next-door to celebrate our survival, even though we didn't have enough money in our travel budget. Up to that point Shelley and I were sharing all the expenses for the trip fifty-fifty, but my cash was running out. Fortunately, she had her checkbook with her, and the hotel and restaurant accepted checks, as neither of us had a credit card at the time. During dinner, we recounted our storm survival experience. We kept looking at each other, huge grins on our faces. Yes, we had some unexpected expenses for the hotel and the dinner, but it was all worth it. We were worth it, as was the special feeling we had about the storm bringing us closer as a couple. We knew we had faced an unexpected, sudden danger and we responded well together, as a team. Now that I look back on that trip, that evening's celebration was one of the best parts.

The next morning, we woke up to a clear and sunny day. When we asked the hotel front desk about the weather report and road conditions to Denver, we were told that the storm was one of those localized, sudden storms that had dumped a lot of snow only in that part of Utah. The interstate had been cleared and we were ready to go. The rest of our trip through Denver and back to Eau Claire was uneventful.

We were gone for about two weeks. We had a good time visiting friends and new places. We saw impressive landscapes throughout Colorado, Utah, Nevada, California, and we also explored the landscape of our young relationship and found it to be enjoyable, interesting, and strong.

Shelley Satterlund in 1975

∗ TWO ∗

Greece, the Beginning

MY FIRST MEMORY IS OF nightmares. They started in 1956, around my second birthday, when we lived in the small village of my birth, Krania, on Mount Olympus. In these dreams, I was always in a jungle with wild animals. All kinds of animals that, later, I learned were lions, elephants, tigers, and others.

In my dreams, I was trying to figure out where I was and why I was there. Many times, one or more of the wild animals chased me, and as one was about to catch up and attack me, I woke up terrified. I was about seven or eight years old in the nightmares, able to run but not fast enough to outrun the animals.

When I woke up, terribly afraid, I left my sleeping spot under the warm blankets on our living room wooden floor and walked the few steps to the bed nearby, where my mother was sleeping. I climbed into her bed and slept next to her for the rest of the night.

My mother slept in the same room with my brother, sister, and me because my father was away, working in construction in the nearby city of Larissa, for five or six days a week. She seemed to understand that I went to her bed when I had a bad dream, and she would help me get under the covers next to her. As I laid beside her, I would place my right hand near her face because I felt safer touching her skin, and it helped me go back to sleep.

I seldom cried during or after these dreams and I could not speak yet. My parents and grandparents were concerned that there was something wrong with me. My hearing was fine, and I understood what they were telling me. Perhaps my speech was delayed because my brother, Yiannis, who was two years older, usually spoke for me. Later I learned that this is not unusual for second-born children. When I started talking, at about three, I had no speech problems.

Around the same time, my wild animal nightmares stopped. I did not tell my mother or anyone else about them. What could I tell them? I didn't know what these animals were. Nobody in our house had ever seen them. We had no radio or television and no books with pictures of them. Where did these creatures come from, and how did they end up chasing me in my dreams?

I was busy learning new words, making sentences, playing, and forgot about the wild animals and the nightmares. However, the memories of them were preserved in my mind and resurfaced when I was in school, learning about the real jungle.

When I was around eight years old, I mentioned my nightmares to my mother and siblings. They thought it was strange and unlikely that I would have dreamt about being chased by animals I had never seen before, and I must have imagined them. Well, isn't that what dreams are? Something that is not real but "imagined" by our minds in our sleep? Our discussion wasn't helping, so I never brought up the subject again.

In high school, when we were studying evolution, I found myself recalling my childhood nightmares again. I began to wonder if our brains contain hardwired images from the early life of humans from many thousands of years ago, when they were evolving in the jungle together with wild animals. Then I learned that lions and other wild animals also lived in ancient Greece, about three thousand years ago, as Herodotus and Aristotle had reported. In Greek mythology, there is a story of the legendary hero, Hercules, who killed a lion in the town of Nemea with his bare hands, but he was not a toddler when he did that.

The only explanation I could come up with was that perhaps certain primitive, threatening images had been passed on to me through my genes. Maybe these vestige images were supposed to be erased before my young brain had started to get organized. Instead, they stayed in my brain longer than usual, and I began to see them in my night-mares. It could be that these jungle images were related to my slow speech development, but I will never know. I am sure, however, that these dreams/nightmares were real.

Other than these early nightmares, my childhood was good. Grad-ually I got to know our neighborhood, the entire village, and many of its residents. In these early years, our small village was my whole world. I wasn't aware of life in other villages, in cities, or anywhere else. I assumed that I would spend the rest of my life in Krania, the same way my parents and grandparents had.

Never in my wildest dreams could I have guessed that my life's journey would take me more than five thousand miles away, to Amer-ica, and that a beautiful girl named Shelley, who had been born there forty-six days before my birth, would become part of my life.

Our village had about two hundred houses. Our house was aver-age in size and similar in construction to the rest of the village. It was built with stone walls about two and a half feet wide and had a red tile roof. There were three rooms on the first floor and three on the sec-ond, and a small wooden balcony. A stairway connected the two floors in the middle hallways.

Our living room was downstairs to the left of the entrance hallway. It had a fireplace, a wooden pantry built against the wall to the right of the entrance, and a single bed set against the pantry on the other side.

In front of the fireplace, we had a small, round table on which we ate our meals. My older brother, Yiannis, my younger sister, Eleni, and I sat on the wooden floor, and our parents and paternal grandparents, who lived with us, sat on short wooden stools.

There was no hospital in the village or in the nearby villages. All pregnant women delivered their babies the natural way, with the help of an old midwife. This worked for most births, but there were cases where babies and mothers died during delivery.

The midwife helped my mother deliver all three of us children, in the living room, on blankets set on the wooden floor, in front of the fireplace. This was the same room we later slept in. In the evening, our mother would spread two layers of thick wool blankets on the floor to act as a mattress and place a sheet on top. She would add one or two softer blankets, depending on the season. It was always warm and cozy during the winter sleeping in this room near the fireplace.

The warm rising air from the fireplace also warmed the rooms above us. In the two bedrooms upstairs slept our grandparents and our parents when our father was home.

The fireplace was the only means of heating the house during the winter. From November to March or April, the fire was almost always on. My mother would start it early in the morning before we woke up and put it out long after we went to sleep.

The house was not well insulated. The windows had a single pane of glass, and the outside door, which was made of wood, was not a very tight fit. On cold winter nights, my mother draped blankets over and along the bottoms of the windows to keep the warm air from escaping and the cold air out. We often heard the cold wind howling outside, noisy, and fearsome, but we felt warm and safe by the fireplace, under the blankets and with our mother's care, love, and her stories. We were probably poor in money and material things, but we were rich in love and attention and I never felt that we were missing much.

The other room downstairs was our storage space. It housed a large wine barrel, farming tools, and served as a chicken coop during the night and goat pen for our six goats during the cold winter nights. The floor was about a foot lower than the rest of the house and made of well-packed soil. The chickens roosted in special wooden shelves my father had installed near the only window, which had a special metal opening and which my mother secured in the evening to keep out the foxes that visited the village at night looking for easy prey.

The storage room had its own door directly to the yard, on the north side, and an inside door in the hallway. Our cooking house was in the yard. It had enough space to keep hay for the donkey, some feed for the goats, and plenty of dry firewood, as my mother used firewood for the daily cooking and for the woodburning oven on the other side of the yard, not far from our outhouse. The cooking house also had a small water tank on the wall with a faucet and a basin below, low enough for us to reach to wash our hands and faces. My mother made sure we washed our faces every morning, with cold water in the warm months and warm in the winter.

Because we used firewood for our daily cooking and for the fireplace in the winter, part of our yard, like all yards in the village, was always covered with large piles of firewood that my father and grandfather brought on our donkey from the forest above our village.

In the smallest corner of the yard, next to the house, my mother put up a triangular-shaped chicken wire fence about four feet high with a wooden door, and she used the space inside as a vegetable garden. We usually had fresh tomatoes in the summer, and lettuce, parsley, and green peppers.

Every Saturday evening, my mother gave us a warm washcloth bath in a large wooden laundry tub. On Sunday, we went to church in our only set of Sunday clothes. Two times each year, our village had a festival, each one associated with a religious holiday; live music played at the village square, where we would buy candy and watch the adults dance traditional Greek dances.

Our village, like most small mountain villages in Greece, at that time, did not have electricity. We also did not have running water or indoor plumbing. We did not miss these conveniences because we did not know what it was like to have them. One of my jobs, starting at about age six, was to go to the village spring, near our house, a couple of times each day to fetch water. I found this an interesting chore because I listened to the women that were at the spring gossiping, as I waited for my turn. Some of them told me that I was a good boy for helping my mother. That made me feel good. I never saw men there because fetching water was considered a woman's job.

My favorite part of the house was the balcony off the second-floor hallway, because from there I could see a bigger world than our small village. It had its own tile roof and, at six feet long by four feet wide, enough space for two adults to sit on two small chairs. For us three children, the small balcony seemed spacious and offered impressive sights and sounds. We felt safe there and protected from the rain.

Our house was located on a major crossroad in the center of the village, and there was always something happening in the streets that met almost directly below our balcony. My siblings and I stood next to each other holding onto the railing, watching the villagers go by on their daily chores. We saw men in their work clothes with loaded donkeys or mules coming home from their fields or vineyards or the forest where, like my father and grandfather, they got firewood for the winter. Others would simply walk by or stand and talk to each other, to our neighbors, our mother or grandfather.

In the warmer months, we watched the clouds move east over the green valley below our village. We knew that a river was meandering leisurely, through the valley to the Aegean Sea, about eight miles from the village, even though we could only see a small portion of it. As I learned more about geography and studied a world map in school, the view of this seacoast became my favorite. I understood that the small part of the sea, visible from our village, was connected to all the oceans and to a much greater world, which I dreamed of seeing some day.

To the southeast, we watched the weather change over the bald summit of Mount Kissavos, which changed colors throughout each day. We cowered at the thunder and cheered the lightning strikes as thick dark clouds moved over the valley in front of us. When there was not much going on below us, or weather worth watching, we talked, sung our favorite songs, played the game "I spy with my little eye," and quarreled for simple and unimportant reasons.

Even though we had cold winters with up to two feet of snow, they never lasted long. January was the coldest month and especially difficult for our animals. On cold nights, our donkey, which usually stayed in the yard, found shelter in our cooking house, and our six goats did the same in the storage room. Some evenings, if the goats, the chickens, or the donkey were not in a good mood, we heard their complaining, sometimes separately, and sometimes all together, creating a big racket. Those irritating sounds forced my mother to drop whatever she was doing and go settle the yellers down. We cheered and clapped when she returned successful from her mission.

My mother, Maria, was in her thirties then, healthy, and strong. She took care of us three children, all the animal needs, plus her daily housekeeping chores and miscellaneous farm work. She cooked for our grandparents and us, fed the chickens and the donkey, milked, and fed the goats, cleaned the yard and the house, and, in the evenings, told us stories. She was very capable and hardworking and made her work seem easy. She never complained except during those very cold winter days when we had lots of snow. Then she would say, "Poor people like us should only have summer. Let the rich people have winter. We need warm weather." This saying usually reminded her of her favorite story, which she told us often because she knew how much we liked it. My mother taught us lots of songs and stories, and we enjoyed all of them. But this was our favorite story:

"Once upon a time, a mother had two daughters. When they were old enough to marry, they married people in two different villages, far away, and she could visit each of them only once a year. The first daughter was married to a crop farmer, and the second one to a clay pot maker. When the mother visited her first daughter, she always complained that they needed more rain for their crops. 'Please, Mother, pray for us to have more rain,' she would say.

When she visited her second daughter, that daughter usually complained that they needed warm and sunny weather so that their clay pots would be safe outdoors, drying in the sun. 'Rain is really bad for our business,' she would say. 'Please, Mother, pray for us to have sunny weather.'

The poor mother didn't know what to do because she loved both her daughters equally and wanted them to be happy. She thought about this predicament for a long time until she finally came up with a prayer that was good for both daughters."

The prayer was in the form of a song that my mother sang for us. The song rhymes in Greek, and it goes like this: "Dear God, please rain, rain long and often, at the place of the farmer, but in the clay pot maker's place, please let it always be summer!"

Every time I heard this story, it reminded me that our mother could well be the mother in the story because she was so smart. I knew that she loved us, and she would do anything for us. And I guessed that she liked to tell us this story as a reminder that all mothers love all their children equally.

Another reason I liked this story was because my mother made it different each time. Sometimes she explained how the clay pot maker's family made the pots and described some of the pots that were placed out to dry in the sun. Other times she would tell us about the daily chores of the farmer's family and the crops they planted, and why they needed rain. It wasn't just a story but a lesson about their professions and how the farmer and the clay pot maker worked together with their entire families to make a living while worrying about the weather, which nobody can control. I understood that our family was more like the clay pot maker's family because we preferred sunny weather and did not like rain or winter.

Most of the year we had pleasant weather in our village. On those days, the dozen or so chickens we had would graze in the neighborhood fields and come home to roost in the evening. The goats went out early in the morning before we woke up. My mother milked them and then guided them to the edge of the village, where they met with the rest of the village goats. From there, the village goat herder and his four shepherd dogs led them to graze on the green hillsides of Mount Olympus. Each household paid the herder annually, according to the number of goats they had.

The herd came back to the village in the evening, and somehow our six black goats would find their way to our yard. I was always surprised to see them coming home. The donkey had his regular spot in the corner of our yard, and in the evening, he munched his hay, staying mostly quiet. Every spring, we would get a small piglet that had the run of the yard and ate our daily leftovers until mid-December, when my father butchered it. We never gave it a name and were not attached to it. We knew from a young age that it was destined to provide meat for the holidays, homemade sausage, and lard for cooking.

You might expect that with the droppings of the goats, the donkey, the chickens, and the pig, our yard would have been dirty and not so sweet-smelling, but that was not so. Our mother always kept it clean.

On the other hand, when we walked the streets of our village, we were exposed to some unpleasant animal smells. The usual source was donkey or mule manure. It was often cleaned by the nearest villager,

The Kyriagis Family in 1959. My parents, Vassilis and Maria, my grandparents, Yiannis and Maria and in front, from the left, myself, my sister Eleni and my brother Yiannis.

but not always. We were used to it and usually jumped over it as a game.

Animal sounds were always present in our yard and around the village. These included our own two roosters and many others from the village, who started to crow early every morning. Throughout the day, we heard chickens clucking, dogs barking, and donkeys braying. All were normal, familiar, and pleasant to our ears. These sounds, together with the laughter and high-pitched voices of happy children playing games, created the rich soundtrack of our daily lives. The friendly tolling of the church bells on Sundays and holidays, and the somber tolling for funerals, added joyful and wistful notes to the soundtrack.

My favorite time was during the warm and quiet summer afternoons, for about two to three hours, when most of the village children and adults would take an afternoon nap. During these hours, the whole village was enveloped in quiet calmness, accentuated only by the sounds of cicadas. I did not nap. Instead, I liked listening to their repetitive summer songs, as they reminded me of the lullabies my mother sang to us when we were toddlers.

Life in our small village had, over many years, developed its own rhythm. The villagers and their animals, like a music band, contributed to the village soundtrack according to their daily activities, which varied with each season and time of day. The sounds were our reminder that everyone was part of the larger community and, for me, the melody of a simple and happy childhood.

* THREE *

Grandmother's Vision

IN MY EARLIEST MEMORY OF my paternal grandmother, I was about five years old. She was named Maria, like my mother, but we called her Yiayia, which is Greek for grandma. One day, as I was walking through our lower hallway to go outside, Yiayia was coming down the winding wooden staircase from the second floor, where her bedroom was, holding an empty looking cooking pot. At the last two steps, she suddenly stumbled and fell slowly to the floor. As I went to help her, the empty pot dropped from her hand. Yiayia closed her eyes, tilted her head backwards, and her whole body started to convulse uncontrollably, including her arms and legs. I froze, as I had never seen her or anybody else in that condition. I called out, "Yiayia! Yiayia! Are you OK?" I knew she couldn't hear me. I was scared something bad was happening to her and started yelling for my mother, who was in the cooking house. My mother rushed in and immediately went to Yiayia. She placed Yiayia's head on her arm and, turning to me, said, "Don't worry. Yiayia is OK. She will be getting up soon. I'm trying to make her more comfortable."

I stood there quietly, scared, and watched Yiayia's face.

Soon after that Yiayia's body started to relax. She regained control of her head, lifted it up to its normal position, and she opened her eyes. She saw my mother holding her and tried to get up. My mother said, "It's OK. Just stay there and rest for a while."

Yiayia lifted her upper body and sat on the floor. She looked around for the pot she had been holding and saw that I had it. Without realizing, I had grabbed the fallen pot when I approached her. Yiayia gave me a half smile and said, "Oh, I see Vagelis [my Greek nickname] tried to help me." My mother answered, "He called me in when he saw you fall down." I kept looking at my grandma's face and at her hands resting on her lap, as I tried to understand what had happened.

The whole incident lasted four or five minutes. Shortly after that Yiayia regained her composure and stood up with the help of my mother. She took the empty pot from my hand, patted me on the head, and walked out the front door and toward the cooking house.

I knew I had witnessed something unusual, but I did not know what. I could tell that Grandma had not slipped and fallen. Or if she did, something more had happened to her in addition to the fall, but I could not figure out what it was.

Later in the evening, I mentioned Grandma's fall to my brother, thinking I had seen something he had never seen before. I was surprised to find out that he had witnessed this behavior in the past. At that point, our mother who heard us talking, stepped in and explained to us that our grandma had a rare condition called epilepsy that caused her seizures and falls.

She said, "Nobody knows what causes it and there is no cure for it. Fortunately, Yiayia doesn't have many seizures, maybe one a week, and they don't last long. But if she has a seizure outside, on rough ground, she could injure herself. That's why she prefers to stay mostly at home. She doesn't like to talk about her seizures, and it's best not to ask her anything about it or talk to other people about it."

My mother's calmness and clear explanation helped me feel better about my grandma's condition. Even though I was relieved that it wasn't more serious, I felt sorry for Grandma. It bothered me that she had to deal with a sickness that made her life difficult. I knew that we had Aspirin in the house that my mother gave us when we had a headache. It wasn't fair that Yiayia couldn't take medicine for her sickness. I was determined to be more helpful to her but wasn't sure what I could do.

Most of the time, we didn't even see Grandma's seizures, as they must have happened in her room. Yiayia had learned to recognize when a seizure was coming, and she tried to find a spot to sit and be safe. After a while, my siblings and I almost forgot about her epilepsy. When we occasionally witnessed a seizure, it didn't frighten us.

Now, sixty years later, I wonder about the impact that epilepsy and its symptoms must have had on my grandma, her behavior, her personality, and her relationship with Grandpa. She was an introvert and a gentle soul, content to be in the background, as her husband was always upfront and in the limelight. He did not seem to worry about grandma's epilepsy, and I never heard him talk about it.

Grandma seldom talked more than necessary. To me, she seemed sad, serious, and dignified. She was thin and of average height and always wore long, dark dresses. Her long hair, which I only remember being gray, was always covered, on the top, in a dark kerchief. I think most people would have considered her plain looking.

Grandma Maria and my grandfather, Yiannis Kyriagis, lived with us or I should say that we lived with them. My grandmother watched our births, helped my mother feed us as babies, and helped us take our first steps. But even though she was always with us, in the same house, for my first ten years, I have few memories of her.

When I saw the first seizure, my grandma was about sixty years old. My mother told us that she had seizures most of her life but did not know when they had started or why. I've learned that even today, in two out of three cases of epilepsy the cause is unknown. About one percent of the population experience epileptic seizures during their lifetime. Now there are medications that limit the seizures plus other medical interventions that make epilepsy easier to live with.

During my grandma's lifetime, no medications or other treatments were available in Greece. Worse, however, was the ignorance and superstition of the people, especially in the villages. People connected epilepsy to demonic influences, and it was considered a mental illness, shameful for the person having it and their families. The common approach was to keep it a secret. To the best of my knowledge, my grandma never had a seizure in public, but I'm sure that our neighbors, and perhaps the whole village, knew of her condition.

In addition to epilepsy, Grandma Maria had a difficult and challenging life. When she was thirty years old, one of her two daughters, Eleni, who was seven, died after a short, flulike illness.

Epilepsy is a neurological disease that has several potential causes, including intense emotional experiences like grief or heavy mourning. Could the sudden loss of her young daughter have caused deep emotional scars in her brain, resulting in epileptic seizures? If the devastating loss of her daughter had not caused Grandma's epilepsy, perhaps it was something she was born with.

I believe that the loss of her daughter affected Grandma's psyche and her personality. In the first ten years of my life, during which I saw Yiayia every day, I do not recall ever seeing her laugh or even smile. She seemed to be in a permanent state of mourning, something today we would consider depression.

Yiayia Maria looked after us three grandchildren the best way she could when our mother was working in our vineyards or potato field or going on her few trading trips each year to the neighboring villages. During those days, my mother left prepared food for Yiayia to serve us when we came home from school. Yiayia took care of us and cleaned the house, but she never helped us with our schoolwork or told us any stories. After a while we learned to accept her as she was.

Neither did she socialize much with relatives, friends, or neighbors. She had only one brother, Dimitris, a farmer who lived in a nearby village and he visited her about once a month. He always brought fresh vegetables or fruit, and Yiayia seemed to enjoy his visits.

When Yiayia wasn't helping my mother, she mostly stayed in her room. On pleasant summer evenings, she would sometimes walk to a spot above the highest house in the village, about five minutes from our house, from where you can see the entire valley of the Pinios River delta, part of the Aegean Sea coast, and the summit of Mount Kissavos. She would meet there one or more elderly women from the neighborhood. This small group sat on flat rocks and talked for about an hour, enjoying the cool breeze and the views of the village and the valley laid out in front of them. Sweet aromas of wild thyme and spearmint mixed with the happy laughter and voices of children playing floated in the air around them.

I cannot imagine what my grandma and her friends talked about. All of them had been born within a hundred yards of their meeting point and had spent practically their entire lives in that village. Were they reliving their early years when they played together as young girls? Or did they talk about the hardships of their lives? Perhaps they were content to just sit together, enjoy the cool summer breeze, and look out as far as their eyes could see, and as far back as their minds could remember. I do know that the time she spent at the lookout point was therapeutic for my grandma. The few times I happened to see her, when she had just returned, she seemed rested and relaxed. I liked to see that on her face.

My parents, siblings, and I moved to the city of Larissa in 1964, when I was ten. For the next few years, during the summer months, our mother and the three of us children went back to the village to be with our grandparents. Our father stayed and worked in the city and visited us on the weekends. My Yiayia was always pleased to see us and to have us home for the summer.

One hot summer afternoon when I was twelve, we were outside, in our yard, and our mother was yelling at my brother and me. "What is the matter with you? You are not small children anymore—you need to grow up," she said with a red face. We were looking at our feet, not saying anything. Maybe she had also slapped us. I do not remember what we had done or not done.

Yiayia was sitting nearby watching the entire scene quietly. She had watched my mother discipline us many times before but had never interfered. This was the exception. Perhaps she felt that either my mother was overdoing the discipline this time, or our behavior was not that bad for our ages.

She interrupted my mother and very calmly said, "Try to not be so hard on them, Maria. They are still young children now, but before you know it, they will be tall young men, wearing suits with white collars and neckties. They will be so handsome and smart that they will make you proud!"

This interference was so unexpected that it surprised my mother and even my brother and me. We looked at each other, then to Grandma and to our mother.

My mother immediately stopped badgering us. She looked into our eyes for a moment with a hint of a smile, and then looking at Grandma she said, "You are right. They will be young men soon enough. I hope that you will get to see them in their suits and white collars." My brother and I were pleased with our grandma's first-time, effective intervention and we grabbed the opportunity and walked out of there.

Later, we realized that we did not know what white collars were. We had seen men with suits and white shirts and ties but had never heard the words *white collar* before. In the evening, our mother explained that white collars were the shirts men wear with their suits.

I was touched by our grandma's words and her vision of us as young men. It seemed to me that she somehow could see the future. Yiayia envisioned us as well-dressed young men and she was proud of us. Her words enabled our mother to see us that way also. When I tried to imagine my brother and me older and wearing suits with white collars and ties, I couldn't do it. Probably because I had no reference point. Few men in our village wore such suits. Besides that, the only pants my brother and I owned were two pairs of shorts for summertime and two pairs of long pants for the winter—one for every day and one for Sundays and holidays. We had no white shirts.

A couple of years after this incident, in 1968, my grandmother died. She left as quietly as she had lived. She had never been in a hospital in her entire life. One day my grandpa sent word to my father that she was sick. My father rushed to the village by bus, as we, like most Greek families at the time, did not have a car. The next day he brought her to the city hospital. She died there four days later. Our family never learned the cause of her death. Yiayia Maria never got to see me or my brother wearing the suits with white collars and neckties that she had so clearly imagined only two years earlier.

Ten years later, in 1978, I started my first professional job. One

My paternal Grandmother, Maria Kyriagis, with my father, in 1948.

day, as I was getting dressed in my navy-blue suit and crisp white-collar shirt and was tying my red tie, I suddenly remembered the vision and prophetic words of my grandma, the "suits with white collars," and an unexpected wave of emotion came over me. I felt a lump in my throat and my eyes tearing. I closed my eyes and saw an image of her face. Along with the sadness for her loss, my heart swelled with appreciation for her love and care for us.

Now I appreciate even more her strength and the quiet, dignified way she lived her life. When I think of her sadness, I wish I could have been more helpful. She has a special place in my heart.

DON'T MARRY AN AMERICAN

The School of the Twelve Gods

IN THE FIRST WEEK OF September of 1960, I was in my very first classroom, as a first grader in our village's only school. Our village had no kindergarten. All children enrolled straight to the first grade in the fall of the year they turned six.

The village is at an elevation of about 2,200 feet, on the side of the foothills of Mount Olympus, nestled among trees and small vegetable and flower gardens and narrow and hilly streets. Most of its two hundred or so houses face south or east, toward the Aegean Sea. The stone-built houses are painted mostly white and have red-tile roofs. They are picturesque and, to this day, convey peace and tranquility. In the 1950s, approximately a thousand people lived there, and about 125 students were enrolled from the first to sixth grades.

I had anticipated my first day of school with excitement. During the previous two years I had watched my mother help my older brother, Yiannis, with his lessons. I listened as he recited the alphabet and watched him as he struggled writing his first letters and words. This exposure helped me learn the alphabet and I could write most letters and even a few words.

On that warm and sunny first day of school, my brother and I put on our clean short pants and shirts, and after a hearty breakfast of goats' milk with homemade bread, we hung our canvas school bags on our shoulders and hopped along like baby goats the hundred or so steps from our home to the schoolhouse.

The school was the largest building in our village, not counting the two churches. It looked like a church to me, with two large classrooms with high ceilings, and narrow, long windows facing east toward the valley and the Aegean Sea.

The first graders, who numbered sixteen total—eight boys and eight girls—sat in wooden school desks next to the windows. Beside the first-grade row, was a row of desks for the third-graders, and on the other side a row for the fourth-graders. Grades two, five, and six were in the other classroom. Each desk had room for two sitting comfortably or three squeezed together. The girls sat in the front desks and the boys in the back. I ended up, with two other boys, in the last desk, which was against the back wall. Fortunately, I got an aisle seat.

On the front wall was a large built-in blackboard and maps of Greece and Europe. On the other walls hung several framed pictures of famous Greek heroes from the War of Independence, from Turkey, which started in 1821.

Our teacher, who sat behind a small desk in the center of the room, was a middle-aged woman, unmarried. Her name was Ms. Eugenia Nikoulis. She was from our village and knew all the students by name as well as our parents, as she had taught many of them, too. She was mostly a dour and demanding teacher. I do not recall her smiling much.

Our school had no clocks. Ms. Nikoulis had a watch on her left wrist and she took it off every day to wind it. Apparently, the watch worked but it did not keep accurate time and it needed a daily adjustment.

One of the first questions she asked our class was if anyone knew how to tell time. I was surprised that I was the only one who raised his hand. My mother had taught my brother and me how to tell time the previous summer. The teacher asked me to go to the village square, about two hundred yards away, where there was a wall clock, to check the time and to come back right away and tell her. I did that on the first day and every school day after that for the rest of the year, and she adjusted her watch. I learned later that it was her custom to select a first grader every year as her time runner. I never understood why she did not buy a new watch. She had no family and with her teacher's salary she could afford it.

I felt responsible and important performing this task every day. I also enjoyed being the only student allowed to walk the village streets while school was in session.

We first-graders started each school day by spending the first hour or so with Ms. Nikoulis while the other two classes were assigned reading or writing. After she finished the first-grade lesson, she gave us an activity to keep busy for about an hour while she worked with the other two grades, which were taught a combination of third- and fourth-grade subjects. She repeated this process a couple or more times during the day.

When I finished my first-grade classwork, I liked listening to the third/fourth-grade lesson. To avoid the scolding, we usually received from the teacher when she caught us paying attention to those lessons, I pretended to look at the papers on my desk.

I usually liked the history and geography lessons. They seemed more serious than the childhood stories and fairytales I usually heard at home. I liked that they were real and about our entire country, which at that time was a new and much bigger concept for me than our small village. My six-year-old mind had started to have a sense of novelty and excitement about learning new things even though I wasn't sure exactly what that meant. This excitement has stayed with me to this day.

I clearly recall the first story that our teacher presented to us on the first day of school. First, she asked us if we knew the name of our village. Everyone raised their hand. "Krania!" said some of us without waiting to be called. Krania is also the Greek name for the Cornelian cherry tree. Around our village these trees grow wild. They make an elongated red fruit, smaller than an olive, and a little sour, even when it's ripe. There are several other villages with the name Krania in Greece, and each usually has a second name to identify its location. Our village is known as Krania of Mount Olympus.

Next, the teacher asked if we knew why the village is known as "of Mount Olympus." Fewer hands went up this time. A girl in the front answered that it was because our village is located on Mount Olympus.

"Yes!" said the teacher, "that is right! We are on Mount Olympus, the highest mountain in Greece. Does anyone know why Mount Olympus is famous other than being the highest mountain in Greece?" she asked.

This time, no hands went up. She waited for a while and then said, "Mount Olympus is the most famous mountain in the world! It's in many books, and most people around the world know about our mountain. They know about Mount Olympus because our ancestors believed in the twelve gods who lived on top of the mountain, not far from our village. In your later school years you will learn about Zeus, the leader of the gods, Poseidon, the god of the sea, Athena, the goddess of wisdom, and about the other gods."

I was surprised to hear this because I thought there was only one god, the one we prayed to in our village church every Sunday, and I had heard many times that he lived in heaven and not on the top of our mountain.

Twelve gods living somewhere above our village! I wondered if any of the villagers saw them when they went to their fields on the mountain or to get firewood.

Why on our mountain? Do they ever come down to the village? Can anyone go and visit them? What kind of house do they live in?

I was so absorbed in my own thoughts and questions that I missed the rest of the teacher's talk. I was anxious to go outside and look up above the village toward the mountaintop to see where the gods could be. When I finally looked up, I didn't see anything different, just the same green hills with trees and the other vegetation.

At the end of the school day, when I went home, I asked my mother if she knew about the twelve gods of Mount Olympus and if she or our father had seen any of them when they had gone higher up on the mountain. My mother said she didn't think anyone had seen the twelve gods as they were part of our history from a long time ago. This did not make sense to me. I thought that since they were called the twelve gods of Mount Olympus, they must still be there. Neither my mother nor our teacher used the word *mythology* that day. And if they had, I don't think that word would have meant anything to me anyway.

Hearing about the twelve gods living near our village, on the very first day of my first school year, made a big impression on my six-year-old mind. It made me think that school was going to be an exciting new adventure and that I needed to understand our mountain's twelve gods. This marked the beginning of my lifelong interest in history, religion, and philosophy.

Today, almost sixty years later, I'm still trying to understand the reasons I was so impressed about the twelve gods. If the teacher was trying to make us feel proud of our village and our country's history and heritage, she succeeded. Even though I didn't know then exactly what pride was, I liked the feeling. This moment became the foundation of my pride in being Greek, which evolved and grew as I learned more about Greek history in my later school years.

* F I V E *

Water, Engineering, & Art

I N MY SECOND-GRADE YEAR, OUR class was combined with
fifth- and sixth-grade students. Our teacher, Mr. Skaramitzios,
was a younger man not from our village. Probably in his late thirties, he was tall and thin with short dark hair and glasses. He seemed
better organized than our first-grade teacher. He was strict but didn't
mind if we actively listened to the higher-class lessons when we finished our work. Every day I raced through my classwork so I could
listen to those lessons.

History and geography were still my favorites. This year the history lessons were more advanced and more detailed. They covered
Greek mythology, including the history of the twelve gods of Mount
Olympus and Greek heroes like Hercules, the Argonauts, Theseus,
Achilles, the Trojan War, and the story of Odysseus's adventures on
his way home from the Trojan War. Much later I learned that these
stories are taught in schools all over the world and are part of the
foundation of Western civilization.

The history class also covered the Greek War of Independence
against the Ottoman Empire that started in 1821. I learned about the
most important heroes and the major battles and struggles over a period of several years, until Greece was finally established as an independent state in 1828.

In geography I learned about our entire country. The mainland re-
gions, the major islands in the Aegean and the Ionia Seas, large cities,

and mountains, rivers, and lakes. I was getting a glimpse of a much larger world than my small mountain village, and I liked that. This exposure, at age eight, made me eager to learn more and understand the physical world of our whole country.

In second grade we had art as a subject for the first time. During our lessons in basic drawing, I discovered that I had zero talent for it. We also had playdough projects. Maybe once a week, for about half an hour, the teacher gave us a blob of playdough and asked us to make something with it. Early in the school year he gave us an assignment to make a house, but he didn't describe what type of house. All the second graders around me started to make a square-looking box, some adding a pyramid-like shape on top as a roof. I wasn't satisfied with that version because it only showed the outside of the house, not the inside space where the people lived.

Because the inside of a house is mostly empty space, I could not figure out how to show that. Finally, after several minutes, I came up with the idea to make a three-dimensional hut that would show the floor, two walls, a simple roof, and the inside space.

I started with a thick layer for the floor, that resembled a triangle. At the long sides of it I attached two walls that were thick enough to stand. Those two side walls connected on the back and were left open in the front. They sloped inward at the top, and there I placed another piece to connect the two walls to resemble a roof. In the center of each of the two side walls I cut a small square opening where I placed a cross-like shape indicating the windows. Inside the hut I put a small square shape and two smaller round ones to represent a table and two chairs, in the back corner a shape that looked like a fireplace, and, above it, on the rooftop, another small vertical shape to represent the chimney.

Through the front open side, the interior was visible as an open space, where the people lived. It was not an impressive house; it was a hut. But it was a fully functioning shelter.

The teacher walked by our desks every few minutes watching me and the other students work but didn't say anything. When time was up and he announced that we had to stop, I had just finished. I was worried that he and the students would make fun of my hut. Some of the students looked at it and snickered under their breath. Then the teacher walked around and inspected our work. As he approached my desk, I had my head down, awaiting his criticism and even his scorn. The teacher carefully picked up my creation, placed it on his left palm, and examined it for several moments.

Then he showed it to the rest of the class, asking if it was a house. Several students said, "No, it's not a house! It's a hut!" Some of them laughed, a disparaging kind of laugh that made me feel embarrassed. I lowered my head again and stared at my empty desktop, feeling my face get warm from embarrassment. I blamed myself for not making a square box like everyone else.

Then the teacher said, "Yes, this looks like a hut, but a hut is also a house because some people live in huts. In this hut, you can see the outside walls but also you can see the inside space, where the people live."

This quieted the students. I lifted my head a little and noticed from the corner of my eye some students picking up their houses and turning them around, trying to see if their house had an inside. I lifted my head higher, thinking that maybe the teacher liked my house.

The teacher then turned to me and said, "I saw you look at the other houses and, at first, you couldn't decide what to make. You had a good idea to try to show the inside space of a house and by making this hut you did that. Well done! You made a good house." He then placed my hut slowly back on my desk.

Turning to the class he said, "You made the outside of a house, and all your houses look the same. Next time, each of you should try to have your own idea of what to make, rather than making the same thing."

The students near my desk looked at my hut with what seemed to me like admiration. At the next school break, several students came to my desk and examined my hut. I held my head high, feeling relieved and pleased that my unconventional approach was a success. I was proud of my creation.

As I think about this art lesson from so long ago, I'm amazed it has stayed in my memory all these years. This is the only clear memory I have from second grade. Perhaps because this was my first experience with taking a risk and getting a reward. It also showed me that it was OK not to follow what others were doing, and to think of my own solution. My teacher's recognition made me feel special and gave me confidence in my own thinking. Maybe this was also the beginning of my appreciation of creativity. It was an important lesson for me, and it had an impact on my later schooling and my entire life.

Going to school and playing in the neighborhood and around the village were our only educational and entertainment outlets. Nobody that I knew, in our village, had toys. We usually played hide and seek, variations of chasing games, played soccer at the village park, and made slingshots to hunt birds.

Sometimes we invented our own games. One fun game we invented is what I call "water engineering." I usually played this game with two or three boys of the same age. Near our house was an open, hilly space that had a small natural spring. The water that flowed out wasn't enough to be useful for watering a garden or anything else, but it was perfect for children's play. Starting at the age of five or six, we usually spent a few hours each summer day pretending to be "water engineers."

First, we would make a small dam close to the spring with stones and dirt and allowed the water to accumulate there slowly. At the same time, below the dam, we built small channels for the water. These had several twists and turns, with variable depths and with bridges made of sticks. We also built other, smaller dams, and a network of more channels, up to fifteen feet long. The objective of the game was to create a flash flood so we could watch how the water moved and interacted with the channels and the small structures we had built.

When our dam at the top was full, we quickly created a large opening so the water would escape downhill with force, flowing into our network of channels and structures. Sometimes, the water moved within the channels and other times it overran them, washing out the bridges and the smaller dams.

Often the water moved with such force that it destroyed all our channels, bridges, and small dams within seconds. Watching this child-made flood and destruction was the most fun part of the game, even though it meant we would have to start rebuilding everything. Or maybe because of it. We were creators and destroyers!

As soon as the water flow returned to the normal, slow rate, at the top large dam, we started rebuilding. We tried to think of new and unusual ways to direct the water flow, new types of structures to build and destroy, and new ways to have fun.

When we were building the water channels and other structures, we had to be down on our knees, focused on each task, talking with each other, arguing about what type of structure to build, exchanging ideas, and working as a team with our minds and hands.

We wore short pants and usually walked and worked barefoot. Not long after we started, we had muddy clothes, knees, hands, and faces. But we didn't care—we were having fun! I wish I had some photos or video of all the intricate channels, dams, bridges, and other structures we created and destroyed. But, alas, nobody in the village had a camera, especially one they'd bother using to photograph children playing in the dirt.

Around noon, our mothers called us to go home to eat. We always left our messy waterworks reluctantly and walked the short distance home knowing that our mothers would yell at us, again, for getting dirty and muddy. My mother helped me wash my hands, face, and knees while complaining that we should not be playing in the dirt and mud. I said nothing, because I knew that the next day, we would be back at the spring playing water engineers again, and I suspected my mother knew it, too.

Our village games were sources of learning and ways to use our imaginations. We learned to have fun, to think creatively, and to co-operate. When I met Shelley and saw her creative side, in playing the piano and singing, I appreciated her talent and her enjoyment of it.

After all these years, I wonder how the creative playing I did as a child affected my approach to life. Like water engineering and my hut from second grade art class, most of my major life decisions have been unconventional, in the full sense of the word.

* S I X *

Grandfather's Three Violins

W HEN I WAS SEVEN YEARS old, my older brother, younger
sister, and I made up this ditty and sang it, in Greek, to irritate our paternal grandpa Yiannis, who lived with us:

Grandpa had three violins.
The first one was smashed to pieces by Grandma.
The second one was stolen by a German soldier.
Nobody knows what has happened to his third violin.

Grandpa's full name was Yiannis Vassilios Kyriagis. He was born
in 1892, in the Greek village of Karitsa, on the eastern side of Mt. Kissavos, looking toward the Aegean Sea. His mother was from Krania, our
village, but for the first twelve years of his life Yiannis had only visited
Krania a few times to see his maternal grandparents. Karitsa is about
fourteen miles from Krania. In those days, over a hundred years ago,
most of the road from Karitsa to Krania was a donkey and mule trail,
half of it on mountain hillsides, that took about five hours to walk on
foot, each way.

At the age of twelve, Grandpa Yiannis became an orphan. He never
spoke to us about his parents or about the circumstances of their
deaths, and we never learned what happened to them. He was an only
child, and his nearest relatives were his grandparents on his mother's

side who lived in Krania and they took him in. After he moved in with them, he spent most of the rest of his life in Krania.

By the age of 12 he finished his schooling and had learned to read and write. At his grandparents' he helped with all the chores around the house and at their few small farm fields and vineyards. They had a few goats for milk and, like most families in the village, a donkey to transport heavy items such as firewood, farm tools, and the grapes during the harvest.

In 1911, at the age of nineteen, Grandpa joined the Greek army to complete his compulsory military service. There he became good friends with a fellow soldier who was a violin player and through him he discovered that he had a talent for music. His friend taught him the basics of playing the violin. He was supposed to serve for two and a half years. But before he was released, Greece entered a period of wars with Turkey and Bulgaria that kept him in the army on and off for a total of seven years, all the way to 1918.

During his military service, Grandpa fought in what is today north-eastern Greece and in several parts of modern Turkey, but he survived and had many stories to share about his army years. Storytelling was his other natural talent. He not only remembered stories, but he created his own humorous anecdotes and poems to entertain his friends and his six grandchildren. His violin playing and colorful and funny stories made him the life of any party.

When he was released from the army, he was twenty-six years old and ready to start a family. A relative suggested he marry Maria Maimaris, who was eighteen years old at the time and from a good family. Yiannis agreed to the arranged marriage even though he didn't know Maria. The dowry that was included in the arrangement was a new two-story, four-room house in the center of the village and a vineyard of half an acre, outside of the village. Yiannis married Maria in 1919, as soon as their small house was completed. A year later, they had a daughter named Despina, and twins in 1923—a son named Vassilis, who became my father, and a daughter named Eleni.

We don't have any photos of my grandparents' wedding. The earliest photo we have of Grandpa was taken when he was about forty years old. He had black hair, a broad forehead, a well-trimmed, thick mustache, a handsome oval-shaped face with a straight, ancient Greek nose, and a strong chin. In the photo he is wearing a sharp-looking three-piece suit with a crisp white collar and tie and holding a fedora hat and gentleman's walking stick. He is looking directly at the camera with a clear and smart gaze, projecting a comfortable-in-his-own-skin attitude and the confident air of a movie star.

I remember Grandpa as an old man. When I was seven years old, he was sixty-nine. He was thin and about five feet eight with no hair on the top of his head and short white hair on the sides. He usually had a pleasant smile on his face and moved around much quicker than his years would suggest. He was still strong enough to work in our fields, cultivating the vineyards and going to the forest with the donkey, in the summer, to fetch firewood for the winter. It seemed to me that he was always talking. With us, my mother, the neighbors, and the villagers passing by our yard, but seldom with our grandma.

Grandpa Yiannis, due to his many years in the army, never had a chance to learn a profession or trade, other than basic skills of tending a vineyard and making wine, which he learned from his grandfather. To support his family, he needed to find ways to supplement the small income from the vineyard and the seasonal general labor he did in the village.

He began to assist the cantors every Sunday at the local church, and within a short time he was good enough to become a regular paid cantor. In the Greek church the cantors perform the task of church choirs throughout the service. By the time he was forty-five, he became the lead cantor of the village; he kept this part-time job for the rest of his life. He was also called to read special prayers at the homes of fellow villagers during funerals and on other special occasions.

On one of his rare trips to the city of Larissa, a day's journey each way, he purchased his first used violin and practiced playing it in his free time. Soon he could play several popular songs of the time, mostly to entertain family and friends.

Yiannis was easygoing, jovial, and worry free. He had no ambition to buy more land or enlarge his house. He was content with the basics for himself and his family and with having a good time with his many friends. Grandma Maria, on the other hand, had higher expectations. She often complained that Grandpa spent too much time with his friends at the local café, and not enough working to provide more for his family. This complaining became more frequent and more intense after Yiannis joined a band that played for weddings and village festivals during the summer and early fall. These festivals usually lasted two to three days, with people drinking and dancing until the early morning hours.

In the beginning, Maria was patient with Yiannis, as he was bringing home additional income from the festivals. But she did not like that he was gone several days at a time and often came home with signs of prior evening heavy drinking.

Yiannis gradually became better with the violin. Having no formal training, he learned by listening to other players. He soon established a name for himself and was asked to play in more weddings and festivals in other villages. Every time Maria complained about his absences, he mentioned the income as his excuse.

In 1926, the Greek government distributed the public land in the valley below our village. This land had belonged to large Turkish landowners as late as 1881, when Turkey still occupied this part of Greece. After the land was annexed to Greece, the government gave each household in Krania six and a half acres. With this land Yiannis learned to be a farmer. The fields had good soil for growing corn and wheat, the two basic crops at the time, but they were located over an hour away from the village. Yiannis, like the rest of the villagers, during the cultivation, planting, and harvesting seasons, walked down to the fields in the morning, worked there all day, and returned in the evening. There was no farm machinery then, only horses or mules and manual labor. Many times during the summer harvest, they spent the night in makeshift huts so they could rest and sleep rather than walk up and down the mountain every day.

For a few years, Yiannis focused on his new fields and only played the violin at weddings and a few village festivals near Krania. But, between farming and playing music, he was away from home quite often.

In the fall of 1930, a family tragedy struck unexpectedly. Seven-year-old Eleni, my father's twin sister, became sick with what appeared to be the flu but with a high fever. The village had no doctor and Yiannis had not been home to appreciate how sick his daughter was. He was at a festival when he received word that Eleni had died. He returned to the village immediately. As soon as Yiannis entered the house and set his violin case on the table, Maria grabbed it, ran outside, and smashed it to pieces on the front steps. Maybe this was Maria's way of saying that Yiannis was responsible for Eleni's death, or of dealing with the loss of their daughter. Or perhaps she had just had enough of him being away from home so much.

When we first heard this story from our mother, my siblings and I cheered for Grandma. Even though we were young, we understood why she was upset. We also felt sad for the death of young Eleni, who would have been our aunt, but we never got to know her.

My mother told us that Grandpa was devastated by the death of his daughter. He went into deep mourning and hardly spoke to anyone during the funeral or for the next few days. He didn't even say anything when Maria burned the broken violin pieces and the wooden case in the yard fire the day after the funeral, to heat water for their laundry. Perhaps he felt guilty for the loss of his daughter and losing his violin was not enough punishment. His silence was probably his way of dealing with his guilt and loss. Losing a child is perhaps the worst thing that can happen to any parent. As a father, I've have always feared such a loss and cannot imagine the pain that it causes.

I never learned how this family tragedy affected Grandpa's relationship with his wife, Maria. I imagine that it must have had a negative effect, because Grandma probably blamed Grandpa for their daughter's loss. Our mother told us that after the loss of Eleni, Grandpa wasn't interested in getting another violin. He seemed to want to spend more time at home with Grandma and their two children.

It took Grandpa Yiannis almost ten years to recover, if it is possible to recover from the loss of a young daughter. In the 1930s, Greece, like most of Europe and the entire world, was going through an economic depression that affected almost everything and everybody. Things did not get better for Greece until the late 1930s. It was around that time that Yiannis purchased his second violin.

Yiannis had to relearn his favorite songs, and this time he also tried to play more songs that his children knew. Maria was not interested in music, but she liked that Yiannis was sharing his music with the children. This violin did not have a case, so Yiannis would hang his instrument from a large nail on the living room wall near the door.

By 1940, Yiannis had started to play with a band again on a regular basis, doing half a dozen festivals a year. The 1940s was to be a disastrous decade for Greece and its people. The problems started in October with an unprovoked war with Italy. A few months later, in the spring of 1941, the German army invaded and occupied Greece.

During the first two years of the occupation, German soldiers did not come to our village. In the spring of 1943, a German supply train going through the valley below the village of Krania was derailed by an explosion. The Germans suspected that the Greek resistance fighters who carried out the railroad sabotage had assistance from the mountain villages above the valley. They ordered German troops to burn all the houses there to force the people to abandon their villages.

The German soldiers came to Krania in May of 1943 without any warning. Many people were working in their fields that day. They were surprised when they saw thick dark smoke coming from all over their village. The soldiers had orders not to kill people but to search for weapons and burn down the houses. They gathered all the men, women, and children and held them under guard in the main square while other soldiers searched and burned down the houses.

When they arrived at our house, Grandpa Yiannis was in his fields. A soldier went inside and found my grandmother, Maria, sick in bed. He found no weapons but saw the violin hanging on the wall and took it.

The soldier probably told his partners outside about the sick old woman inside the house and they decided not to burn it down. Maybe they thought that taking the violin was punishment enough.

By the end of that day, most of the houses in our village had been burned. The houses were all built with thick stone walls. However, the key part of stone houses are their roofs. The roofs were made of wood with red clay tiles on top. The soldiers threw small pouches of explosives on the roofs that penetrated the clay tiles and set the wood on fire. When the beams burned, the roofs collapsed inward onto the second-story wooden floors, as most houses had two stories. Then the floors and everything on them burned, leaving only the four stone walls. Without the second-story floors and the roofs to keep them together, these free-standing walls would collapse. Indeed, only a few houses survived—some by accident, as the fire went out before serious damage was done, and some due to owners being bedridden inside.

When the villagers returned from their fields, they found themselves with nothing left but the work clothes they were wearing, and their fear and despair. The German soldiers forced them to abandon the village before nightfall. Most went initially to live with relatives in nearby villages, and later made the one-day's walk to the city of Larissa to live in temporary shelters established in schools or at abandoned military bases. They were refugees in their own country. These were probably the most difficult years for our family and everyone else in the village, and in Greece.

When my mother told us this story, my immediate reaction was to look at the large nail on the wall next to the door. It was still there, holding nothing. I tried to imagine Grandpa's violin hanging there, but I couldn't.

I had seen a musician playing a violin at one of our village festivals, from some distance away. I knew what a violin looked like. For many days after my mother told us the story, I wished that one morning I would wake up and find a violin hanging by the nail on our living room wall, but that never happened.

I asked my mother about her house. She looked sad when she told us she was seventeen years old when the Germans came and remembered the day well. She was in one of the vineyards with her parents and siblings when they saw thick dark smoke covering the entire village. They left the vineyard, and as they approached the village they saw German soldiers with guns standing sentries in a few high points. They were afraid and didn't know what to do. Her father knew that the Germans were burning the houses and thought that if they went to the village, perhaps they could salvage some of their things. He guided them carefully and quietly through the thick vegetation of a ravine that led to the village.

In the village, they saw many houses already burned and people running around, scared, crying. When she saw their own house, there was only four darkened walls standing. Inside were smoldering flames here and there. Nothing could be salvaged. They lost everything—any money her parents had in the house, all their clothes, and all their household goods. The only parts that were not burned were their cooking house and a storage shed in the yard, where they kept tools, and the feed for the donkey, goats, and chickens.

My mother almost cried when she talked about that day. She said, "I was really scared. It was the worst day of my life!" When I heard that, I got mad at the German soldiers and felt sorry for my mother and her family and the whole village. The stolen violin was no longer on my mind.

Grandpa accepted the loss of his violin relatively well. He considered himself fortunate that his family was not hurt, and that the house was not destroyed. He mentioned to us once that he thought his violin probably saved our house. He imagined that the soldier who took his violin was a violin player himself and did not wish to burn down the house of another violinist. I thought that the German soldier was a thief, even if he was a violin player.

The rest of the 1940s continued to be difficult for our village and for Greece. After the German army left in 1944, the village was rebuilt with materials supplied by the government.

A couple years later, Yiannis was able to buy his third used violin and he started to play in a band again at festivals in nearby villages for extra income. Maria got upset every time Yiannis played at a festival and tried to get him to quit. Yiannis didn't want to give up his music and kept his violin at a friend's house for safety.

As small children, living in the same house as Grandpa Yiannis and Grandma Maria, we heard stories about my grandfather's violins from my mother, but we never saw Grandpa play or heard him talk about the violins. We never understood why.

Our mother told us what had happened to the first two violins, but we had never learned what happened to the third. We searched all over our house for it but didn't find it. When we asked our mother and grandma what had happened to it, they would say go and ask your grandfather. He would only say, "I don't remember," and changed the subject. But we were kids and couldn't resist irritating Grandpa every now and then by singing our little ditty about the three violins.

When we were children, Yiannis was our favorite grandpa. We liked his easygoing and mostly pleasant personality. He enjoyed spending time with us and telling us stories, both serious and funny, and giving us money to buy candy. But as we grew older, we learned that he was not a good provider or ambitious enough to improve his family's finances or save money for the future, including his retirement. He was more interested in having a good time and seldom missed an opportunity for free drinks. His public persona was that of a happy-go-lucky person with no worries other than entertaining his friends. His behavior as a father and husband did not measure up to what was expected of him by his family.

When we were older, our father made it clear to us that his major goal in life was to not be like his father, whose behavior he considered inadequate, and at times, even embarrassing. But he always treated his father with respect and made sure he had enough cash to buy clothes, cigarettes, and coffee at the village coffee house.

At some point we got tired of asking Grandpa what had happened to the third violin and almost forgot about it. After we moved to the city of Larissa in 1964, Grandpa Yiannis and Grandma Maria stayed behind in Krania for a few years. When my grandmother died in 1968, Grandpa moved to Larissa to live with us. We asked him then, a few more times, about his third violin and he gave us the same old answer.

Grandpa Yiannis died in 1975 at the age of 83 in our house in Larissa, while I was a university student in Wisconsin. I assumed then that we would never find out the fate of the third violin. Many years later this assumption would prove to be wrong. I'll get to that later.

My Grandfather Yiannis Kyriagis with his son Vassilis and his daughter Despina, in 1930.

SEVEN

The Immigrant Grandfather

MY MATERNAL GRANDFATHER, EVANGELOS MATOS, was known as "the American" for most of his life. He spent sixteen years in America as a young man, and after his return to Greece, his fellow villagers gave him this nickname.

When I was old enough to have a real conversation with him, at about age seven, my grandfather was seventy-one years old. He lived with my grandmother, Katerina, in our village, about a hundred yards away from our house. He was a tall, handsome, wide-shouldered man with short, silver-white hair. I have my grandfather's first name and have been told that I inherited a good share of his personality.

You might think that someone like him, who had spent so many years in a faraway and famous country, would have many stories to tell. Unfortunately, he did not. On the other hand, Katerina, my maternal grandmother, who had never been outside her village for more than a few weeks in her entire life, and who had only a fourth-grade education, was a fountain of stories and songs.

This telling of my grandfather's life is based on stories I've heard from my grandmother Katerina, my mother, other relatives, and family friends.

The defining event in my grandfather's life was his immigration to America in 1909, when he was eighteen years old. He was an only child who became an orphan, as his mother—Maria Sorfa, from the nearby village of Pirgetos—died from complications during his delivery. After his mother died, his father was unable to look after him, and he was raised by his maternal grandparents in Pirgetos until he was about fourteen years old. During these years he didn't see his father very often. It must have been difficult growing up with his grandparents, without a mother or father. I suspect that this probably affected his personality and behavior later in life like it did for my paternal grandfather, Yiannis.

Evangelos went to elementary school in Pirgetos, and all his first friends and early childhood memories were from that village. He saw his father a couple of times each month, and at first, he seemed like a stranger to Evangelos. When Evangelos moved to Krania to live with his father, and his stepmother named Penelope Karasimou, he had some difficulties adjusting to life in Krania, but thanks to his stepmother's love and attention, it didn't take him long to adapt to his new life. Many years later, when Evangelos started his own family, he named his first child, a daughter, Maria, after his birth mother whom he never knew, and his second daughter Penelope, to honor his stepmother. When he was about eighteen, a small group of young men from the village started planning to go to America to work. Two of Evangelos's friends were among the group and asked him to join them. Evangelos's father, Giorgos, did not want his only son to go to America and tried to change his mind. After missing his early years, Giorgos liked having his son living with him.

Giorgos was industrious and hardworking. He cultivated his own vineyard that produced grapes for wine and ouzo and raised silkworms on the second floor of the house. In the winter months and his other free times, he worked at his loom, which he'd built himself in the lower part of the house, making blankets and other household items.

Evangelos was a tall, athletic, and strong young man. He liked helping his father in the vineyard and with other outdoor chores but was not crazy about feeding the silkworms or working at the loom. He detested the loom. He would rather work outdoors than be shut in the house.

One of his best friends was Mitros Tzatzas, who was two years older than Evangelos, also tall and well built. Mitros came from a poor family and was prone to small animal thefts. He had started stealing chickens in the village as a prank and roasting them at picnics with his friends. Later he moved on to stealing goats and sheep from the nearby villages of Pirgetos and Rapsani and sold them at low prices to opportunistic butchers in other villages.

Mitros had not yet gotten in trouble with the law, but people in the village knew what was going on and rumors about his stealing were spreading. He had his first legal problems when he enlisted in the Greek army to serve his mandatory military service. He got into a fist fight with one of his superior officers and went AWOL. The police came to the village, arrested Mitros, and took him away to Larissa with his hands tied behind his back.

Evangelos's paternal grandfather was a retired teacher who lived in Pirgetos. He had heard the old men in the village coffee shop discussing Mitros' arrest and the rumors that he and some of his Krania friends had been stealing chickens and goats. He said nothing at the coffee shop, but he was concerned about his grandson's friendship with Mitros.

About a week later, Giorgos was visiting his father and told him that Evangelos was among a group of young men preparing their immigration papers to leave for America in the fall. He added that he wanted to stop his son from going.

Giorgos's father told him that he would be making a big mistake if he stopped his son from going to America. He said, "There's another big war coming soon. Greece is going to fight with Turkey again. If Evangelos doesn't go to America, he will be enlisting in the army next year to serve his mandatory service. What would you rather have, a dead son from the war, or a son alive in America? You should let the boy go. This is the right thing for him to do at his age. He will avoid the war and America will be good for him. He will also make money, and in a few years, he can come back to marry a local girl. Besides, I hear that he is friends with Mitros Tzatzas, who's a thief and a troublemaker. Staying here is not going to be good for Evangelos."

Giorgos wasn't sure what was the right thing to do. He probably felt guilty about not being a real father for the first fourteen years of his son's life. Now he was looking forward to Evangelos getting married and having grandchildren. He thought about the advice of his father, who read books and newspapers and considered what the future may bring. If a war was coming, he didn't want his son to be in the army. He had also heard the rumors about Mitros Tzatzas and knew that Mitros was a bad influence on Evangelos. As Giorgos walked behind his loaded donkey, for the one-hour trip on the uphill trail to Krania, he made up his mind to follow his father's advice to allow his son to go to America.

Evangelos was pleased to hear that his father had changed his mind, even though he did not tell him why. He suspected that the change had something to do with his father's visit to Pirgetos.

Evangelos spent the rest of the summer taking care of his immigration paperwork and looking forward to the trip to America. He had never been further than the nearby villages.

Some of the villagers were envious of the six young people going to America, and others were sad because they didn't know if they would ever see them again. A few people who had left Krania in previous years to go to America had never returned. Some were never heard from again. No one knew for sure if the future would be better for those who were leaving or those who stayed behind.

There have always been people who choose to go to new, faraway places. Immigration is seldom, if ever, a search for adventure. It is most often an act of desperation, based on the hope that the faraway, unknown life will be better than present living conditions. Perhaps this is how humanity makes progress.

In the first week of September 1909, the small group of young men left Krania, each with a single suitcase. Friends and relatives followed them to the edge of the village, from where they could see them off as they took the downhill trail leading to Pirgetos.

In Pirgetos, Evangelos stopped to say goodbye to his grandparents. He first visited his maternal grandparents who had raised him. Both cried and told him they wished he would stay in his village. His grandmother held a small package tied up in a large cotton napkin, which Evangelos knew from its aroma contained freshly cooked spanakopita—spinach pie—his favorite food. She handed it to him crying and asked him to be careful and to write. Evangelos took the warm cloth napkin in his hands and hugged and thanked his grandmother, in tears. He assured her that this was the right thing for him to do, said not to worry about him and that he would write often.

Then he visited his paternal grandparents. His grandfather, also named Evangelos, told him he was glad that he had convinced his father to let him go to America, because he believed it was the right thing to do. Then he said, "Take good care of yourself, and in a few years, when the time comes to marry, you must come back to marry a Greek girl from Krania or Pirgetos. Don't marry an American!"

Evangelos laughed and said, "I promise you, when the time comes, I will come back and marry one of our girls, but I am in no hurry to get married."

As his grandfather said goodbye, he hugged him and kissed him on both cheeks and then gave him a white handkerchief with a knot at one corner, as it was customary for Greek grandparents to do, bulging with what young Evangelos knew was folded money. "This is for the trip," his grandfather said, crying. "I've been saving it for you. Don't forget to write to us when you arrive in America."

Evangelos wiped his eyes quickly and thanked his grandfather and grandmother. He didn't know then that this was the last time he would see any of his grandparents. All four of them died while he was in America. I know how he must have felt— because three of my four grandparents died while I was in America.

He rushed to catch up with his Krania friends who had been waiting for him at a coffee shop on the main road. They walked to the train station another half an hour away. Around noon, Evangelos and the five young men from Krania boarded the train for Athens. They arrived just before dark and spent the night at a cheap hotel near the train station. The next morning, they took another train to Patra, a port city on the northwest side of the Peloponnese peninsula. There they boarded the SS *Alice*, and after three weeks, with stops in Naples, Italy, and Marseille, France, the *Alice* arrived in the port of New York.

I have a copy of a piece of paper that was left by Evangelos in his handwriting, in Greek and in English, indicating that his ship arrived

From the right, My paternal Grandfather, Evangelos Matos, Yiannis Baslis, (his business partner) and an unknown friend, in 1925.

in New York on September 28, 1909. His passenger record at the Ellis Island American Family Immigration History Center shows his date of arrival as October 1, 1909, most likely because it took him two to three days to go through the immigration process before being officially admitted to America. Evangelos stayed in America for the next sixteen years, until 1925.

My "American" grandfather almost never talked about his years in America. He earned a reputation as a man of few words. He preferred quiet conversations with a few friends and was not among the village square coffee shop regulars, not even during his retirement years. He avoided large groups and heated discussions of all types.

It is difficult to know why he didn't share the experiences of his sixteen years as an immigrant in America. His reluctance to talk about his life there reminds me of people who have returned home after a terrible war, like World War II or Vietnam. It's as if they're trying to forget the agony and pain of witnessing death and destruction all around them.

Were my grandfather's years in America as difficult or as deeply affecting as a destructive war that causes PTSD? I do not know. But I imagine that those years had an impact on him for the rest of his life.

About fifty years after he left America, I found myself in America and my life changed, in ways I could not have imagined. Unlike my grandfather, I am pleased to share what I learned about his story and the experiences of my life in America.

EIGHT

A Greek Marriage Proposal

O N A COLD AND WET Saturday evening in March of 1951, Vassilis Kyriagis, who was to become my father, was about to act on the most important decision of his life. He had decided that he wanted to marry a young woman from his village named Maria Matos. That evening, he was going to Maria's house to ask her parents for their permission. This was a difficult task because he knew that Maria and her parents were not expecting his visit nor his marriage proposal.

I learned this evening's details, and what followed, from my mother, who liked to tell this story. Our father never talked about it.

The standard procedure of the time was to send a trusted relative to the potential bride's parents to express interest on the groom's behalf and to negotiate a dowry. This had to be done secretly and quietly to avoid gossip and embarrassment in case the bride's family refused.

Vassilis had been thinking about his task for some time, trying to figure the best way to carry it out. He knew that his father, who was known for his love of drinking and long stories, wasn't the right person for the job. He reviewed in his mind the short list of people who might represent him well and decided that the matter was too important to leave in someone else's hands.

Twenty-seven-year-old Vassilis was about five feet nine inches tall, with a lean body and a strong build. He had thick black hair, a dark complexion, a handsome face, and a pleasant smile when he used it.

He combed his hair toward the back of his head as was the custom of the time. He had a steady job as a construction worker in Larissa and was known as a serious man. He minded his own business, avoided gossipers, and watched his drinking and his public behavior. His request to marry Maria Matos could be turned down, and that made him nervous and uncertain. He worried that he was not good with small talk or any talk.

Vassilis was probably more mature than other men his age, due to the three years he had served in the army during the Greek Civil War, which followed the German occupation. He fought in several major battles against the Communist insurgents, in the mountains and near his village. He lost several friends in the war. Being close to death for three years, he learned to appreciate the important things in life. The hardships he experienced in the war made him a stronger person and even more serious. He also developed leadership skills in the army and was promoted twice, reaching the rank of sergeant.

By March of 1951, Vassilis had been out of the army for almost two years. He had saved some money and began to build a two-room addition to his parents' house so that he could start his own family. In the previous few months, he had started to consider potential wives from among the young women he knew from the village. He wanted a woman from a good family who was serious and dressed and behaved modestly.

Maria Matos's house was only four houses from his, less than a hundred yards away. Over the past year, he had seen her in the village many times, either in church or on the street. Sometimes he saw her sweeping her entryway as he walked by on his way to the village square to the coffee houses. At about five feet seven inches, she was on the tall side for a woman, with a thin but strong physique, a good-looking oval-shaped face, and long brown hair. She carried herself with confidence and strength. When they passed each other on the street they greeted each other using the standard greetings: "Good morning," or "Good evening." Any more talk would provide fodder for gossip and was frowned upon by the elders.

Even though he never had a real conversation with her, Vassilis concluded that Maria would be a good lifetime partner, and a good mother. He knew her family and liked her reputation as a "good girl." If a girl of marriageable age had been "talked about," her chances of a good marriage were greatly reduced. Maria met Vassilis' expectations of a potential wife. Perhaps there was some physical attraction, but I doubt that it was love in the modern sense of the word.

On that March evening of 1951, Vassilis sat at one of the coffee houses in the village square, trying to gather his thoughts and the strength he needed to walk over to Maria's house, unexpected and uninvited, to ask for her hand in marriage.

He had a strong coffee with friends and waited to get dark outside so he could walk to Maria's house without being seen. If the villagers saw Vassilis visiting Maria's house, a man going to the home of a woman of marriageable age, there could be gossiping next day.

Vassilis considered having an ouzo to fortify his courage, but he decided against it. He wanted to have a clear head and a smooth tongue. When it was dark enough outside and he felt ready, he said goodbye to his friends and left the coffee house.

As he started to walk toward Maria's house, which was close to the village square, a light rain had restarted. When he arrived, he looked behind casually. Seeing no one on the street behind him or in front, he quickly took the dozen or so steps uphill and entered Maria's yard, then a few more steps to reach the front door. He was nervous, but ready to present his case.

He knocked, and in a few moments Maria's mother, Katerina, opened the door. Before Vassilis had a chance to say anything, Katerina said, "Oh! Vassilis, *kalispera* [Good evening]. How are you? Come inside so you don't get wet."

Vassilis was standing under the balcony above the main entrance. "*Kalispera*," he said, "it's not raining much. I wanted to talk to Vagelis, [Evangelos's short name, Maria's father], if he's in."

"Yes, Vagelis is inside. Come into the main room, he's sitting by the fireplace."

Vassilis walked through the hallway to the main room, where he saw Vagelis by the fireplace and Maria sitting on a bed that served as a sofa during the day, working on a needlepoint lace. He said, "*Kalispera sas* [Good evening to you both]!"

Maria said "*Kalispera*," and immediately stood up and put her needlepoint on the bed, having no idea what was about to happen. She then left the room to go to the kitchen, which was in the yard, to get a glass of water and something sweet to serve Vassilis, as the local hospitality custom required. She assumed that Vassilis had come to talk to her father about something related to one of the vineyards or perhaps the herd of goats that her two younger brothers were raising with the help of her father.

While Maria was in the kitchen, Vassilis immediately started to talk to her father and mother. He pointed out that they knew him and his family, so there was no need to talk about that. He then told them that he had decided the time had come for him to marry and start a family. He explained that he had known the Matos family for long time, being neighbors and all, and that he thought Maria was a fine young woman who would be an excellent wife and had come to ask their permission and blessing for their marriage.

Vagelis and Katerina were surprised, as this was totally unexpected. For a moment they didn't say anything, they just looked at each other. When they recovered from the awkwardness, Vagelis said, "Yes, Vassilis, we do know you and your parents well, being neighbors and all. And we know that you are a serious, hardworking young man who has fought for our country. We certainly want to discuss your request with Maria because she is the one who should decide this important matter."

Katerina nodded several times as Vagelis spoke but didn't say anything. Such conversations were considered men's talk.

Just as Vagelis finished speaking, Maria walked in with a tray of homemade sweets and a couple glasses of water. She held the tray in front of Vassilis. He looked at her with a smile and said, "Thanks. I will not take a sweet but will take the water."

Maria then offered the tray to her father and he took the other glass. She left the tray on a table and, looking at her father, she asked, "What is it that I should decide?"

Vagelis explained that Vassilis had come to ask for her hand in marriage. Now it was Maria's turn to be surprised. She knew that the time had come for her to marry. She was almost twenty-five. Under normal conditions she would have been married already, but due to the civil war and, before that, the German occupation, the villagers' lives had been disrupted in the worst possible way. Maria's house was among those that had been burned by the Germans. And then during the Greek Civil war that last three years, she and her siblings became war refuges again to Larissa for more than a year.

It was only in the last year or two that the lives of the people of Krania were getting back to some normality. Some young people had gotten engaged and even married. Some of Maria's relatives had suggested potential suitors from their villages, but Maria immediately put a stop to those discussions. She wasn't ready to marry as her family was still trying to recover from the wars. Besides, when the time came, Maria wanted to marry someone from her own village. Maria loved Krania and did not want to be separated from her family and friends. When she had to live as a war refugee in Larissa, away from her home, she was quite unhappy. Maria believed strongly in prayer, and in the power of the Virgin Mary to answer her prayers. She prayed often to be able to return to Krania. When a woman in Larissa offered to arrange for her to marry someone from that city, Maria realized that she could no longer assume that she would live in Krania for the rest of her life. She knew that she would marry someday, but it was not certain that her future husband would be from Krania. She had prayed fervently to the Virgin Mary that when the time came for her to marry, the Virgin Mary would find her a husband from Krania.

And there, in her house, was a potential groom from Krania, asking her parents, in person, for her hand in marriage. She was flattered, but also surprised and unsure what to say. She felt her face warming up and was sure she was blushing. Her mind raced but no words came to her. She just looked at her mother, then at Vassilis, and finally at her father with a blank expression.

At that moment, Katerina noticed that Vagelis seemed unsure what to say, so she said to Maria, "This sure is a very important decision,

Maria." Then she looked at Vassilis and with a smile added, "We hope you can give us some time to consider this carefully, Vassilis, before we give you an answer. Can we give you our answer tomorrow?"

"Yes, of course," Vassilis said. "I realize that my visit was unexpected. I am here in the village working on the house addition. When you make your decision, perhaps you could come over to the house to let me know. As for a dowry, that is not important to me. Whatever you're planning to offer as Maria's dowry is fine. It is Maria that I came to ask for in marriage and not her dowry."

This impressed Maria. She believed that most men put too much emphasis on the dowry, and that the reason they sent someone else to discuss the possibility of marriage was to negotiate the dowry without making the groom look bad. She thought, *Right here, this evening, Vassilis came to my house and asked for me to become his wife and he does not even care about the dowry!*

Vagelis assured Vassilis that it was their responsibility as parents to provide Maria with a dowry, even though the wars were hard on their finances. He added that they would discuss that later, after Maria made her decision. He then thanked Vassilis for the honor of asking them for Maria's hand in marriage and assured him that he would have their answer the next day.

Vassilis thanked everyone for their hospitality and, after he shook everyone's hand, including Maria's, walked out of the main room as Katerina escorted him to the door. "You picked a good time to come," she said. "It's dark out and the rain is keeping people indoors, so they won't see you leaving our house."

"That's what I thought," said Vassilis. "I hate to give people reasons to gossip." He wished Katerina goodnight and walked out the front door and disappeared into the darkness.

Katerina locked the door and returned to the main room to find her husband and daughter sitting quietly, thinking. "That sure was an unexpected visit," she said, as she tried to suppress a mischievous laugh.

"Yes, that was unexpected!" said Vagelis, "but I give Vassilis a lot of credit for coming in himself and not sending someone else to talk to us. He seems to be a serious man. And I hear that he's an awfully hard worker."

He looked over to Maria, who seemed to be in deep thought. Katerina noticed that and asked, "What do you think, Maria, about Vassilis?"

Maria looked up at her mother first and then at her father. She told them that when they were in the refugee camp, she had prayed to Saint Mary that when the time came to marry, she wanted to stay in Krania, and not marry someone from another village. It seemed to her that Virgin Mary had heard her prayers. Maria now had a marriage proposal not just from someone who lived in Krania, but from someone they knew well, from their own neighborhood, close to their home.

Vagelis was not religious. He asked Maria to think about this proposal and not rush her decision. "It's best to sleep on it, Maria," he said, "and we can continue our discussion tomorrow."

Katerina nodded, "Yes, that's a good idea. Let's all go to sleep, and we can talk about this again in the morning."

Maria couldn't sleep that night. The unexpected proposal forced her to examine her whole life. She knew the time for marriage had come and she should not delay it. Even though she had not considered Vassilis before, as a potential husband, she couldn't find any reason to say no. He was a serious and good-looking man. Even though his family didn't have much, Vassilis was a hard worker, and he was expanding their house in anticipation of his marriage. Maria liked the idea that her potential new home would be close to her parents' home, and that she would be able to see them and her siblings any time she wished. She believed that Saint Mary had indeed performed a miracle. Before she finally fell asleep, she decided that her answer would be yes. She would accept Vassilis's proposal and marry him.

The next morning over breakfast, Maria told her parents, quietly so the younger children wouldn't hear, that she had decided to marry Vassilis, and her mother should go over to his house later that day, after church, to give him their answer. That afternoon, Katerina placed a block of feta cheese on a plate, covered it with a cotton napkin, and walked the short distance to the Kyriagis house. The previous night's rain had stopped, and it was sunny and warmer. Vassilis saw Katerina coming, and after a brief greeting in the yard, he escorted her inside where his parents were sitting. Katerina gave them all a big smile and said, "I bring good news. We are happy to become one family! Maria has said yes! We are happy to have Vassilis as our son-in-law!" After warm embraces by everyone, they worked out the engagement announcement and celebration details.

It was decided that the wedding would take place in December of that year, so that the Kyriagis house addition would be completed, and the Matos household would have enough time to prepare for the wedding. Vassilis was told that Maria's dowry was a vineyard of half an acre, six of the best goats from Maria's family herd, and a small amount of cash. Vassilis and his parents accepted it courteously.

That same evening, Vassilis, with his parents and his sister, Despina, and her husband, Giorgos, visited the Matos house after dark for a small, informal engagement party with feta, olives, wine, and fruit. The next day, they announced the engagement to their neighbors, relatives, and friends.

After the announcement, Vassilis and Maria could be together in public without concerns about gossip. Vassilis visited the Matos house when he could, and Maria visited the Kyriagis house and got to know her future in-laws, with whom she would be living after the wedding.

During the months of their engagement, my mother got to know Vassilis and felt confident that they would make a good couple. She was an extrovert, always quick with a greeting and smile, and made friendly, easy conversation with people she knew and those she had just met. Maria had many ideas and needed to talk about things, while Vassilis was happy to listen and think carefully about the options before he made decisions.

The wedding took place on December 23, 1951, in Krania. Vassilis and Maria had their first son, Yiannis, in October of 1952. I was born in October of 1954, and my sister, Eleni, in June of 1956.

When my siblings and I asked our mother if she loved our father when they got married, she told us that they developed a special and strong love for each other. This love matured as they lived together through difficult times and through the many joys of raising their family. Over the forty-six years they were married, it was obvious to all who knew them that they had a deep and unwavering love. They were able to communicate with a simple look. In all the years I knew them, I don't recall any arguments or cross words between them. Maria was very much in charge of the household's everyday decisions, but she made sure that everything was done with Vassilis's knowledge and approval. She treated Vassilis as the head of the family and the household, who had the last word on all decisions. Vassilis respected Maria's ideas and initiatives and had full confidence in her abilities as a mother and as manager of the household finances and the family.

I believe that their life together was one of enduring love, respect, and mostly happy times, an example and inspiration for their children and grandchildren.

NINE

Vinegar Sweeter than Wine

MY MOTHER, MARIA MATOS KYRIAGIS, was born in Krania in 1926. Her first sixteen years were about as good as they could have been at her village that time. She was the oldest of five children and received plenty of love and attention from her parents and grandparents. She attended the local elementary school, where she excelled as a student. At thirteen, after she finished her sixth and final grade, she started to help her mother around the house and assist her younger siblings with their schoolwork.

Her idyllic and worry-free life ended when she was seventeen. In the spring of that year, in 1943, German soldiers came to the village and burned most of the village houses including hers. After the German army left Greece in 1944, my mother's family returned to the village and, like most of the people, started to rebuild their house and their lives.

Three years later, in 1946, as the villagers were making progress rebuilding their houses and their lives, the Greek Civil War started. Soon Communist insurgents, who used the mountain above our village as a hiding place, started visiting the village in the middle of the night and knocking on doors.

These were rough men with dark beards and weapons who inspired nothing but fear in the people. Initially, they asked only for food: bread, cheese, olives, whatever the villagers had. People had no choice but to give them what they asked for. Later, the communists started to force boys and girls as young as fifteen to join them to fight with them against the Greek army.

When the forced recruitment started, my mother, who was twenty-one years old, her four younger siblings, and all the other young people of the village were moved by the Greek army to Larissa as war refugees and forced to live in crowded old military barracks for more than a year.

My mother and her siblings had to live in one room, and they were given one free meal per day, usually soup. Fortunately, her two brothers, Giorgos and Grigoris, who were nineteen and fifteen, respectively, were able to get some work in the city doing general labor and anything else they could find, earning barely enough for food and clothes for their family of five.

Maria's parents stayed behind in the village to look after their small herd of goats, which was their livelihood at the time. When the civil war ended in 1949, Maria and her siblings returned to Krania. Two years later Maria married Vassilis and moved into his house, to live with him and his parents, Yiannis and Maria.

Vassilis and Maria were a good team. Vassilis's construction job kept him away from his family five or six days a week, working in Larissa. Maria managed the household and, together with our grandpa and occasionally our father, cultivated our two small vineyards and a potato field. These fields provided a good part of our family's income.

Our two small vineyards, about an acre together, produced grapes for the family to eat as fresh fruit from mid-August to mid-September. The rest of the grapes were made into wine and ouzo for our own household but also to trade in other villages for staples like dry beans.

In the late 1950s and early 60s, there was little cash in circulation among villagers in Greece. There was also high inflation due to the recent war, and people preferred to barter their goods rather than using cash.

Most of the people in our village either farmed small plots of land, like small vineyards, or grew potatoes and other vegetables. Our village and neighboring Rapsani have the right climate for vineyards. The grapes and wine were traded in the village above us, called Kallipefki, which sits at too high an elevation for vineyards. However, that village produced a lot of dry beans, which is the national food of Greece and the most important staple of the Greek diet.

Fall was the trading time for potatoes and beans. Starting in late September, my mother, with the help of my grandfather, loaded our donkey, the family's only transportation, and set out before the first daylight for one of the nearest villages to trade the potatoes for dry beans. My mother arrived early, traded her load quickly, and returned home in time to do her daily household chores.

Where there is a market, a natural form of competition follows. It is this competition that sets the price range and determines who will trade his goods faster and with better terms. Maria was outgoing and had a quick and pleasant smile and a powerful memory. She listened to her customers and paid attention to their stories. She remembered their names and their relatives and used that in her conversations. When she traded with a new client, she would ask about their relatives and friends in the village, their names and where they lived. Then she would visit these relatives and tell them that so-and-so sent her to them because they wanted them to have these "good potatoes or wine" that Maria was offering for trade.

Maria "advertised" her products with a pleasant, clear voice, saying things like "Come and get the best-tasting potatoes you've ever had. You get three kilos of potatoes for only one kilo of beans." Her product knowledge, her excellent customer relations skills, and her pleasant personality helped people enjoy talking to and trading with her.

On top of her natural talents and skills, she discovered a powerful secret weapon for trading. She genuinely believed that in a trade, both sides should feel satisfied. She traded the best potatoes her field produced. When she weighed the potatoes, she made sure that her scale leaned in her clients' favor. After completing the exchange of goods, she would thank her clients, saying something along these lines: "It's so good that we traded today, and I appreciate your cooperation. I want to make sure that you get a fair deal, so let me throw in a few extra potatoes." Then she would reach into her sack with two hands and place a handful of potatoes in the client's container.

She discovered that most of her clients liked this gesture and usually reciprocated by putting a handful—with both hands like Maria—of dry beans into her bean sack. Maria didn't know that this is a natural human tendency that social psychologists call reciprocity. When someone does something nice and unexpected for us, we want to reciprocate the good deed out of a natural sense of fair play, to feel good about ourselves.

At first, Maria did this from her innate sense of fairness and for her customers' satisfaction. Soon she discovered that the handful ratio of beans to potatoes was much better for her than the normal barter rate of one kilo of beans for three kilos of potatoes. At the end of the day, Maria ended up with more beans than others trading at the standard rate. She believed that the extra beans she was getting were a gift from God, a reward for being honest and trying to do what was right and fair for her clients, and she accepted the "gift" without telling anyone about it. She made this gesture of fairness a standard practice in all her trades.

In 1960, I was six years old, oblivious to most things, including my mother's talents and hard work. She was thirty-four years old, healthy and strong. She had three children, ages four, six and eight.

She took about a dozen day trips per year to nearby villages, to trade potatoes, fresh grapes, wine, and ouzo, for beans, lentils, apples, and chestnuts. She usually woke up at five in the morning to load our donkey with over two hundred pounds of potatoes with my grandfather's assistance. Then she and my grandpa or one of her sisters, with our donkey, would walk anywhere from one to three hours to one of the neighboring villages. There she walked the village streets for about two hours, trading her load, and when she was finished, they walked back to our village with the donkey loaded with about eighty pounds of beans or other traded items.

In the fall of 1963, Maria and Vassilis were excited about the expected bountiful grape harvest. Earlier that year Vassilis had started building our new house in Larissa in a lot he had purchased the year before. They were hoping for a good wine year to earn more money than usual to cover the extra expenses of our new house.

Winemaking was a joint project for Vassilis and Maria. They followed the fermentation process very carefully, using sulfites to prevent oxidization and kill the bacteria. Our wooden barrel was so large that it could not fit through our storage room doors. It had to be built in the room by a local cooper at great expense. With a capacity over a thousand liters, it occupied half the room. It had a large opening on top and one in front. At a certain time, after the fermentation process, both these doors had to be sealed one hundred percent tight to prevent the vinegar bacteria, known as Acetobacter fermentation gases, from entering the barrel. These bacteria are always present in areas where wine is fermenting and are the greatest enemy of wine producers, even more so at that time when wooden barrels were not as reliably sealed as the stainless-steel tanks are today. Maria and Vassilis had made wine in that large wooden barrel for almost ten years—they knew the process and their wine was good.

That November of 1963, after the fermentation was completed, Maria and Vassilis added the sulfites and sealed the barrel. However, the sealant they used, made with flour, was not of the right consistency and didn't stick properly to the doors of the barrel. They had to redo it two or three times. Even then, they weren't sure the seal was reliable and there was no way to test it. When Vassilis came home from the city on weekends, he inspected the sealing material and added more sealant a couple of times. They wouldn't know if the wine was safe from the vinegar bacteria until next spring when they tested it.

With the excitement of the holidays, her family responsibilities, and other household chores, Maria did not seem to worry about the wine until February when it was time to test it. Relatives, family friends, and other people in the village had started to report that they were tasting their new wine and that it was ready for consumption and sale. Maria, with the help of our grandfather, Yiannis, drew some wine to test it. Grandpa said it tasted somewhat different, but it was OK. Maria, like most village women of that time, had never drunk wine or any alcoholic beverages in her whole life. She wasn't sure what good wine tasted like.

In February of 1963, when I was nine years old, I was mostly preoccupied with playing with my friends and with schoolwork. I first sensed that that something was wrong in our house when I noticed that my mother was asking my grandfather to taste the wine almost every day, and she carefully watched his face for unusual grimaces.

She didn't say anything to us about the wine. I saw her take some to her parents' house and assumed she had asked her father to taste it. I heard my mother instructing my grandfather, in hushed tones, not to mention anything about the wine possibly going bad to anyone in the village. The family's reputation was on the line and until they were sure what the problem was, and what to do about it, he was to keep quiet.

I did not understand what the problem was, but I could tell that it had to do with the wine and that it was serious. Next Saturday, when my father came home, my mother offered him some of the new wine during dinner. When he tasted the wine, he didn't say anything about its quality, perhaps because he didn't want to have the discussion in front of us children. My grandfather tasted the wine again and insisted it was fine. On Saturdays, my mother was usually cheerful, because our father was home, but I noticed a worried look on her face.

The next day, after the Sunday church service, and after the main meal of the day, my mother's mother came over, anxious to find out what Vassilis had decided about the wine. For some time, my mother, her mother, my father, and grandfather were in the storage room with the wine barrel, and I could not hear their discussion. For the next few days, I didn't hear anything about the wine, but I noticed that my mother had stopped offering new wine to my grandpa to test. I assumed that whatever problem there was must have been resolved. My mother, however, still looked preoccupied.

Her mother visited us one evening that week. She usually came to spend some time with us children, to tell us stories or bring us a special dish. On the way out, by the main door, she had a quiet conversation with my mother, which I couldn't hear. I guessed that they were whispering on purpose, which seemed unusual as my grandmother normally didn't linger when she was ready to leave.

Later that week, I heard my mother say to my grandfather, "There is nothing we can do about it. The whole barrel has turned to vinegar, and it is the worst thing that could happen. It is embarrassing! The whole village will start talking about us behind our backs and laugh at us. The money we expected to earn from this barrel is now gone! It's a disaster!"

My mother told us later that she knew that some people were envious of her trading success and secretly wished that some misfortune would befall her or her family.

My grandfather, who was usually optimistic and easygoing, said, "Don't worry. This has happened to other people before. It's not the end of the world. We will think of something."

My mother said, "I worry about the cost of a new barrel and what we're going to do with so much vinegar. I cannot get this off my mind!"

I learned later that when wine turns to vinegar, the barrel is damaged forever because the vinegar bacteria are impossible to remove from the barrel walls. It can no longer be used for wine, only for vinegar.

The next day, my mother took some of the wine to her mother and asked her to use it in any dishes that called for vinegar. She had to find out how good it was to use as cooking vinegar, so she could sell it as such. We had over a thousand liters of it and, even if she gave some to all our relatives and friends, there was no way all that vinegar would be used up. We would probably have to throw a lot of it away, as quietly as possible, and she hoped that the people in the village would not find out.

Our grandmother, Katerina, came to our house the next day and announced that this was "very good vinegar!" She asked my mother to keep at least ten liters for her. On her way out the door my grandma, joking, added with a laugh that the situation wasn't a total loss. At least she would get some good vinegar. That evening my mother was quieter than usual and I imagined that she was still thinking about the vinegar problem.

The next day was Saturday, and my father came home. After the main meal, my mother explained to my father and grandfather, while us children were still in the room, that both she and her mother had used the vinegar a couple of times in dishes, and they agreed that it was very good. She would not throw it away. It was bad enough that they had to replace the wooden barrel. Her plan was to try to sell the vinegar in the coming week to her best clients in Kallipefki.

My father and grandfather were surprised. Nobody from the village had ever tried to sell or trade vinegar before. People bought vinegar in small quantities as needed, at the local grocery store.

My father asked, "Do you think people will buy our vinegar? What price would they pay for it?" Before my mother could answer he added, "You know that the whole village will find out about the wine failure and it will be embarrassing."

Maria said that she had been thinking about all these questions and decided that embarrassment was not the biggest problem, after all. The biggest problem was how to trade the vinegar, as it was something she hadn't done before. But she believed that it could be done. Every household needed vinegar, even the households that don't need wine. People used it to preserve their olives and other vegetables. They also used vinegar in salads and other dishes and for cleaning and disinfecting. Maria hoped she would be able to sell some vinegar to many households, and since everyone else from her village would be selling wine, she would not have any competition.

She convinced my father and grandfather that it was worth trying to take a load to Kallipefki to test the market. The following Monday, she and my grandpa would go with a donkey load of six twenty-five-liter containers of vinegar.

To my grandfather's surprise, things turned out much like Maria had hoped. While there were several other traders selling wine, our mother with grandpa were the only ones selling vinegar. The grape season was so good the previous year that there was an oversupply of wine and the price was lower than usual. Maria decided that her price for the vinegar should be the same as the price of wine. And to my grandfather's amazement, they sold their whole load within the first two hours. When they returned home that afternoon, their entire faces were smiling. My mother couldn't wait to tell us what had happened. After they unloaded the donkey with the beans and other traded items, and she checked to make sure we were OK, she rushed over to her mother's house to tell her parents about her successful vinegar trading day. They were pleased to hear the good news. They knew Maria had been worried about this. They also believed that if anyone could do what she had just done it would be Maria.

That evening my mother told us the whole story for the first time. She told us about her worries that the wine had to be thrown away, how relieved she was that she would sell the vinegar, and that everything was going to be OK.

By Saturday of that week, when my father came home from the city, about half of the vinegar had already been traded. My father was surprised, impressed, and pleased as he listened to my mother and my grandfather describe what had happened. I could see that my mother was happy and we, the children, sensed that this was an important celebration of success for our family.

In the next couple of weeks my mother and grandfather completed their trading trips and sold the rest of the vinegar. She had already given to her parents and other relatives some and kept some for our use. It was more than we would normally use in a year. My mother said that this was the sweetest vinegar of all. I could not understand how vinegar could be sweet, but I believed my mother.

This family ordeal made a big impression on me. Today, more than fifty-five years later, I can still see the worry on my mother's face over this problem and her relief and joy when it was resolved.

How do parents teach their children not to give up easily when problems arise in their lives? I raised two sons and found that hard to do. I don't remember my mother ever telling us not to give up or to use our knowledge, talents, and skills to solve our problems. I think that children often observe their parents' and grandparents' expressions and behavior more than they realize. I may not have understood all the issues involved with the vinegar problem, but I was receiving clues and lessons from the actions of my parents and grandparents, from the emotions painted on their faces, and their gestures.

My mother, most likely, had not realized that when she was trying to figure out what to do with one thousand liters of unwanted vinegar, she was teaching her children the value of creativity, determination, and persistence.

The vinegar of 1963 was the last vinegar or wine our family made.

The year after that, two things happened that made wine-making obsolete for us, as well as for most families in our village. That year, a new cooperative winery opened in the village below ours, and most people in the village started to sell their grapes to the cooperative rather than make their own wine. The buying prices for the grapes the wine cooperative paid were not high enough, but the vineyard owners had an alternative to making their own wine.

This period was also the beginning of the Greek domestic migration. Many villagers had started to move to the cities for better jobs, for their children's higher education, and for better living conditions, such as indoor plumbing and electricity. My father had finished the house he was building in the city, and we planned to move there later that summer.

The Magic of Electricity

LIFE DURING MY FIRST TEN years in the village of Krania was idyllic. A simple life, with no cars, city noises or pollution. We had a safe and warm home and plenty of food. We had parents and grandparents who loved us and told us stories. The school was close to our house and mostly fun. My siblings and I played with our friends almost every day, at school and in our neighborhood.

From the beginning of 1964, my mother started telling us about the major move we were about to make as a family to a new house that my father had built, in the city of Larissa, about twenty miles to the south. I had no idea what city life was like because I had never been to one. Mother had been there before, and she was preparing us by emphasizing the conveniences we would have in our new house.

She said that the most amazing new thing would be electric light. In the village, we used an oil lamp to light our living room. The lamp was small and not very bright, but we were used to it. We did our schoolwork with it, sitting on the wooden floor in front of a low round table on which we also ate our meals.

"You'll be amazed how bright the electric light is in Larissa!" my mother told us. "The light comes from a small, round lamp that hangs down in the center of the ceiling and it never needs to be filled with oil. You press a button on the wall and the light comes on, like magic. And then you press the button on the wall again and the light turns off."

I believed that this would be magic. "But how can a lamp work without oil?" I asked. I had watched my mother fill our lamp with oil almost every day. I figured that every lamp must need oil to give light. "If the lamps in the city don't need oil, why don't we get that type of lamp for our house in the village?"

"Well," my mother said, "the lamps in the city don't work with oil, they work with something called electricity! And it is only available in the cities. Every house pays for the electricity; it's not free."

I couldn't imagine how those lamps worked. I tried and tried to understand the magic of electricity, but I found it impossible. I counted the days until I could see this magic for myself.

We moved to Larissa in late August of 1964, about two weeks before the new school year was to start. We took the bus; it was the first time we were on a bus and we found the ride exciting and fun. My father had arranged for our household items and a bunch of firewood to be transported by the village tractor. Our grandparents continued to live in our village home.

Our city house was at the edge of the neighborhood, next to open fields. There was a dirt road in front of our house and, next to that, wide open fields. The ones next to the road were not cultivated as they had been sold as lots for future houses. Further out we saw dried remnants of harvested crops, maybe wheat or something similar. About two to three hundred yards away was the straight line of the national freeway, with vehicles moving in both directions. There was no traffic on our street at that time, as hardly anyone in our neighborhood had a car. Everyone got around on bicycles.

I was not impressed with our new house, as it looked small to me. At one story high, it wasn't as big as our house in the village. It was built with bricks and had only three rooms next to each other—a living/dining/sitting room, a bedroom for our parents, another bedroom for us three children—and a small kitchen attached at the end with its own lower roof. Our bathroom was in the yard, just like in the village. But we did have electricity and running water, which were big improvements, and we liked that.

We had a big enough yard for us to play in with space for a small vegetable garden. A year after we moved, my father built an addition to the house. It included a separate dining/sitting room, a patio, a hallway connecting the new rooms to the older house, and a bigger and better kitchen. He converted the original kitchen to a larger and better bathroom with a small tub and a shower. I liked our new, bigger house much better then, even more than our village home.

When we first arrived at our city house, I couldn't wait to see the electricity. When I entered the house, I saw the lightbulb hanging two feet below the high ceiling. My mother pointed at a small white button near the door and asked me to press it. I pressed the button and the lightbulb turned on. I pressed the button again and the light turned off.

My mother watched my face and saw my amazement. "You see?" she asked, smiling. "It's like magic. You press the button, and it goes on and off."

I said, "Yes! It is like magic!" and I kept pressing the button on and off, hoping that it would not work, but the light kept going on and off. I called my sister, Eleni, to come and see the magic light. She came running, and after I showed her how the button worked, she took over and kept pressing it. My mother walked by with an armful of our belongings and told us to stop and help her.

For the first couple of evenings, I remember looking at the light and noticing how bright it was—it lit up the entire room. "This is much better than our village lamp for sure!" I told my mother. My brother and sister agreed.

Within a few days, we forgot about the magic of electricity and started to take it for granted. Life is like that. The most amazing things we see for the first time can soon seem ordinary. The same thing soon happened with the running hot and cold water. It was new and interesting only for the first few days.

Soon we started to experience other city wonders. We went to a city square and saw a water fountain with lights that changed the color of the water in the evening, as we watched sitting on nearby wooden benches. We saw professional photographers in white coats standing beside large cameras on tripods taking photos of well-dressed people. We had our family portrait taken by one of them and it was ready within an hour. We went to a movie house and watched a movie for the first time. On October 28, we saw a large parade celebrating Greece's victory over Italy in 1940. The parade lasted over an hour and included police cars, fire trucks, marching soldiers and army tanks and other military equipment we had never seen before.

We were impressed with all these new things and liked them all. But again, after a while we started to take everything for granted. We came to understand that we were in the city now and all cities had these things. I decided that I liked our new life in the city better than our life in the village.

When school started, it didn't take me long to get to know my classmates. The school was close to our house, and several of my classmates lived in our neighborhood. Established a couple of years before, the school was small and used a large two-story house for its classrooms rather than a typical school building. There were about one hundred students, including about twenty in my fifth-grade class.

From the very first day of school, every time I said something in class, the other students looked at me in a strange way. The teacher explained to them that I had just moved to the city from a mountain village and my accent was different. In the village we usually dropped the last vowel or two of longer words so we could speak faster.

Even though the teacher told the students not to make fun of the way I talked, some of them repeated my pronunciations and laughed. I was surprised because I talked the same way everyone in our village talked. I did not think I was doing anything wrong, strange, or funny. After all, I was speaking the same language. Anyway, I decided it was best to imitate the other students' way of speaking. This turned out to be easy to do, and a few weeks later my village accent was practically gone. I had no idea at the time that in the future I would be speaking a foreign language with an accent for the rest of my life.

Around the same time, I realized that the fifth-grade lessons were easy for me. Within the first month, it became obvious to the teacher and the students that I was ahead of the rest of the class. I was always raising my hand to answer the teacher's questions, and my answers were usually correct.

Most of the time, in fact, I was the only student raising my hand. The teacher, who was a jolly, overweight man in his late fifties or early sixties, one day said to the class, "Why is it that this student who came from a small mountain village seems to know the answers and you who grew up in the city don't?" Nobody had an answer to his question. I started to think that even though our village didn't have the comforts or magic of the city, we must have had a good school, good teachers, or both.

By this time, the other students had stopped making fun of my accent. At the end of the school year, I was among only four students who received a grade of ten, the highest grade in the Greek elementary school system. This top grade reinforced my pride about coming from a small village. When I finished sixth grade also with a final grade of ten, I was certain that my village experience had been an advantage.

By 1969, when I was fifteen years old, my adaptation to city life was complete. I was old enough by then to go to the movies with friends, to the city center and city squares, to shops and parks and the library, to the soccer stadium to watch games, and to enjoy the good things that a city like Larissa offered a teenager.

Larissa is the largest city in the region of Thessaly, and its history goes back nearly five thousand years to ancient Greece. Because the plain of Thessaly is the largest in Greece, it has always been the center of Greek agriculture. In addition to producing the major agricultural products, like wheat, corn, oats, cotton, and others, it was also known for raising the best horses, the most famous being Bucephalus, which belonged to Alexander the Great. Bucephalus was an exceptionally large, strong, and swift horse, black in color with a large white star on its head and is credited for saving the life of Alexander many times, during his long military campaign from Greece to India.

The people of Thessaly had a reputation for being good farmers who enjoyed an easy and comfortable life but had few artistic or cultural pursuits. One might consider Thessaly a cultural backwater of ancient Greece.

Later in my life, during my university years, Greece was becoming an internationally popular tourist destination, and people I knew in

America would often ask me what the tourist attractions of Larissa were. I usually told them that most tourist guides had a sentence like this about Larissa: "Larissa is the largest city in Thessaly and an agriculture and business center of the region. You may skip it without missing anything."

Then I would share the story of Socrates's trial by the city of Athens in 399 BC. We know from the books written by Plato, that Socrates, who was then seventy-one years old, was found guilty of "failing to acknowledge the gods of the city [the twelve gods of Mount Olympus]," and for "introducing new deities." He was sentenced to death by drinking the poison hemlock. In the very early hours of the day he was to take the poison, several of his wealthy and influential friends visited Socrates in jail and informed him that they had bribed the guards, and everything had been arranged to have him transported to Larissa where he could spend the rest of his life in comfort and safety. In my humorous version of this story, Socrates responded, "I would rather drink the hemlock than spend the rest of my life in Larissa!"

Socrates's real answer, of course, was different. He refused to escape because that would be against the laws of the city, which he respected, and against his own philosophical principles. He had nothing to say about living in Larissa.

The people of Thessaly and Larissa can still take pride in their history as home to at least a couple famous, ancient heroes. The legendary Jason and his Argonauts, who around 3000 B.C. successfully sailed to the shores of the Black Sea to obtain the Golden Fleece, came from a place near Larissa.

Achilles, the greatest hero of the *Iliad* and of all ancient Greece, was also from a town near Larissa. His participation in the Trojan War, around 1100 BC, was instrumental in the Greek victory over Troy.

In recent years, Larissa, finally, found a tangible way to appear in a positive light in the tourist guides. In the late 1970s, while digging the foundation for a commercial building downtown, workers discovered the remnants of the city's ancient theater, built in the third century BC. The city purchased all the properties on and near the theater site and over a period of over twenty years excavated the entire theater.

The theater is now in the process of reconstruction and restoration, and in a few years will be ready for live theater and music performances. Located in the heart of the city, it is large and in fairly good shape. It has become a major tourist attraction for Greek and foreign visitors, and the pride of Larissa and its people. Larissa now has a direct cultural connection to the glory of the ancient Greek heritage, is proud to show off the theater to the world, and to have earned a positive entry on all current tourist guides.

After my first couple of years living in Larissa, in the mid 1960s, I was pleased to be living there and proud of how well I navigated my new life. I thought about all the wonderful city things that my old classmates and friends from our village were missing. I was convinced that Larissa was the right place for me and pleased that it was my home. I believed then that I would be happy to spend the rest of my life there. I did not realize that ten years later I would leave Larissa and end up spending the rest of my life very far from it.

* ELEVEN *

Foreign Exchange Student Dream

I N THE SUMMER OF 1966, soon after the end of my sixth grade, a letter came to our house from a private English-language school in our city, congratulating me for my perfect final grade and offering me one year of free English lessons, three per week for one hour each. I asked my parents' permission, and they were pleased to accept the offer.

At that time, Greek middle schools and high schools offered French as the only and mandatory foreign language. It was well known that French was on its way out as an international language, and many small private English schools had sprouted in the city offering lessons at reasonable rates. I found French difficult, to say the least, and after my first free year of English lessons my father was pleased to pay the fees to let me continue.

Two years later, in the fall semester of 1968, I learned from my English teacher, Mike Sophiadis, who was Greek, about an opportunity to go to America as an exchange student through the AFS Foreign Exchange Program. AFS Intercultural Programs began in 1915 as the American Ambulance Field Service, which provided American ambulance drivers to Europe during World Wars I and II. The writer Ernest Hemingway, was one of the volunteers AFS drivers in Italy, during World War I.

After the end of World War II, AFS transformed itself into an international secondary school exchange organization. The goal of AFS was to build a more peaceful world by promoting better understanding among cultures. Students from around the world, who were in the eleventh grade and spoke English well enough to attend the senior class of an American high school, were eligible to apply. Those who were selected were placed with American volunteer host families for about a year. All expenses were paid by AFS—the students' families paid only the amount they were able to contribute.

Learning about AFS was an important turning point for me. Even though I had made progress with my understanding and writing of English, I was becoming frustrated by my poor speaking fluency. I thought the AFS program was the right opportunity for me to become fluent. Plus, it offered the attraction of living for a year in America, the land of new technologies and most of the movies I watched in local theaters.

I thought that going to America would be like moving from our mountain village to the city. Even though moving to the city was a little difficult at first, it didn't take me long to adapt and enjoy everything city life offered. I knew America was a lot further, and I thought I would probably have some language problems, but the things that I would see and learn in America would be worth the difficulties.

In September of 1968, when I was barely fourteen years old, I made the decision that when I was old enough, I would apply to go to America with AFS and complete my senior year of high school there. Every semester after that, I asked Mike, who continued to be my teacher, about the program—what qualifications were required, what tests I had to take, etc. He assured me that he would keep me advised on everything. He seemed pleased that I was eager to become an AFS exchange student.

In 1969, I learned that Mike's younger sister, Theodora, had been accepted in the program and was already in America. Mike told me that he had learned a lot more about AFS through his sister's experience and planned to use this knowledge to help his students.

The time for me to apply came in the fall of 1970, when I was sixteen. Mike had explained in detail the entire selection process. First there was a written test to determine your level of knowledge of English. Then there would be a personal interview by the local AFS Selection Committee.

If one passed the first two steps successfully, their file would be sent to the AFS main office in New York. From there the student files were sent to American families interested in being hosts. If an American family agreed to host a specific student, only then would the student be accepted by AFS to go to America.

In the fall of 1970, as I prepared to apply, I was not worried about the details of the AFS selection process. Instead, I was concerned about the fifty Greek drachmas that was required by AFS for the application fee, —money that I did not have. This amount is equivalent to $1.75 in 1970 dollars, or one third of my father's daily net pay as a construction worker.

I asked my parents for the money and explained why I needed it. This was the first that my parents had heard about the AFS program and what it meant to me. My mother immediately jumped up and said, "You must be kidding us! You have no business going to America and staying with a foreign family for a year at such a young age. Even if you passed the tests, we would never let you go. Why throw away fifty drachmas for the tests? Just forget about it and mind your schoolwork."

I was not surprised by my mother's reaction. She was usually overprotective of us. But I thought that I could change her mind. I tried, calmly, to explain to my parents the benefits of the AFS program and the school year in America. I told them I wanted to be fluent in English and that if I spent a year in America, I would be able to pass the test and earn the English certificate of proficiency, which would qualify me to become an English teacher in a private English school. I patiently explained that the proficiency test is almost impossible to pass without studying in either England or America. They did not seem impressed, nor interested. It was obvious that my mother was not going to change her mind in that moment. I decided not to push my luck and to work on convincing my father later, without my mother present.

I talked to my father a couple of times alone in the yard while my mother was inside cooking and explained that the application deadline was coming up. He asked what was the total cost our family would need to pay for the program and the application process. I summarized everything as best I could. He was still not ready to commit to giving me the fifty drachmas, but as the deadline approached, I kept badgering him about it.

Then, a week before the deadline, as we sat on our patio, my father informed me and my mother that he was giving me the money. Turning to my mother, he said, "Chances are good that he won't be accepted. I'm willing to give him the fifty drachmas so he'll stop asking me every day and won't be able to say to us in the future that we prevented him from going to America for fifty drachmas."

My mother seemed surprised. She pursed her lips and looked first at my father and then at me and said nothing. My father took out his billfold and handed me a fifty-drachma note and said, "Here are your fifty drachmas." I took the money eagerly, thanked him, and walked away quickly, before my mother tried to change his mind.

In October of 1970, thirty-two students from Larissa, with a population of about eighty thousand, took the AFS English-language written test, and nine passed. Among the nine were three of Mike's students, Nick, Sue, and I. We knew each other well, and because of our common interest in AFS, we were becoming good friends.

A month later, we had our personal interviews with the AFS Selection Committee, which was comprised of previous AFS students and headed by an AFS representative from Athens. The questions were meant to evaluate our English-speaking ability and get an idea of our personality and adaptability. I talked about my experience of moving to the city from our village when I was ten, and I think this probably worked in my favor.

Soon after that, we found out that of the nine students interviewed, four were selected to send their files to Athens and from there to the AFS offices in New York for final selection by the American host families—Nick, Sue, and I, from Mike's school, and Katerina, from another school. The files we prepared contained information and photos of our families, our responses to a long questionnaire, and letters of recommendation from teachers and others.

On the advice of Mike, we visited our city's mayor's office and asked him to write us a letter of recommendation along the lines of a sample letter that Mike had given us. The middle-aged, overweight mayor seemed pleased to meet us and hear about AFS. As we were talking, he handed the sample letter we gave him to his secretary and asked her to prepare three letters for his signature. The letters were identical, except our names. Mike knew that they would go to different files within AFS and to different USA families, so no one would notice that they were similar.

I remember that the first sentence of the letter was something like "I was very pleased to learn recently that so-and-so has been accepted by AFS to attend high school for a year in America and want to assure you that he/she will be an excellent representative of our city and our country in America."

We also included a glowing letter of recommendation from our English teacher, Mike, and I was able to get a letter from my father's army veteran association. All these letters were written to appear spontaneous and glowing in their tone. AFS Greece translated them into English and placed them in our files that went to New York City. Then I waited anxiously, for about five months.

In April of 1971, a letter from the AFS office in Athens arrived at our house informing my parents and me that I had been selected to go to America and would be hosted by the Howard and Marguerite Wagenbach family in Barron, Wisconsin. What an exciting and memorable day!

I could not stop smiling and walking around our house and yard with the letter in my hands. My mother saw my excitement and wasn't sure how to react. I guessed that she was waiting for my father to come home from work. When he did, and I told him the news, he said, "Good for you!" and nothing else. I guessed that he expected that my mother would not be happy.

As we were standing outside on the patio, my mother came out and said to my father, "Did you hear the news? It's your fault for giving him the fifty drachmas!"

My father didn't answer her right away. Eventually he said, "Let me wash first and have a glass of water and we can talk about it later."

I guessed they probably had mixed feelings, because they realized that their prediction, or perhaps desire, that I would not be accepted did not turn out to be a good strategy. But their pride for my acceptance to the program probably muted any concerns they may have had. I felt confident that they would not stop me from going to America.

In the days after the letter's arrival, I could tell that my parents were still not sure how to feel about my going to America, and whether they should allow me to go, even though they saw how pleased and excited I was. I hoped they felt it would not be right to deny me this opportunity after I had made the final cut.

Finally, a week later, they grudgingly acquiesced and told me they had decided to allow me to go. My mother reminded my father a few times, mostly joking, that if anything bad happened to me in America, it would be his fault. He retorted that I had earned this opportunity fair and square, and the right thing to do now was to wish me good luck and a safe trip and stay in America.

With natural parental pride, both accepted the fact that their second son, at the tender age of two months shy of his seventeenth birthday, would be leaving home to live with an American family for almost a year!

I was thrilled that I had made the final cut! I read the letter many times over. Wisconsin? I kept asking myself. I had never heard of that state before. I went to the public library and looked up where it was. At first, I was a little disappointed that I wasn't going to a better-known state like California or New York or Texas, states that almost everyone I knew had heard about. They were in the movies. But Wisconsin? Nobody had heard of Wisconsin. A friend asked me, "Do you mean West Kansas?" "No!" I said, "It's different than West Kansas. It is WIS-CONSIN!"

I didn't mind that Wisconsin wasn't famous. It was still America. It must be exciting! And they speak the same language.

That same week Nick and Sue received their letters. Nick was going to La Puente, California, and Sue to Osco, a small village in northern Illinois. Later we learned that Katerina was going to Long Island,

Nebraska. In 1971, thirty students from Greece, out of about three thousand students worldwide, were selected to go to America, live with an American host family, and attend the local high school as foreign exchange students.

A couple weeks later, I received the first letter from my host family. It had photographs and information about the family, their four children—John, Teresa, Kim, and Kathy, and about their farm and the town of Barron.

The news that my host family lived on a farm outside of town didn't surprise or bother me. One of the questions we had to answer in the application was whether we would mind if our host family lived on a farm. Mike had advised us to respond that not only we would not mind, but we would welcome the opportunity. He knew that many American host families were farm families from smaller towns and our chances for placement would be greater if we were willing to be hosted by a farm family. Sue was also to be hosted by a farm family. I owe Mike a debt of gratitude for his guidance in the AFS selection process.

My views of American farms were based on the American movies I had seen. I enjoyed being in the countryside and I expected that I would like the wide-open views. I started to envision myself as a cowboy, riding on a horse and leading the cows on a cattle drive.

I exchanged a few letters with my host family. My English wasn't good enough at that time to write long letters, but I told them about my Greek family, pictures of whom they had already seen in my AFS file, and that I was looking forward to being in America, living on the farm with them, and attending the local high school in the same grade as Kim, my American brother.

When I told my Greek classmates that I was going to America next August, and that I wouldn't be in school with them next year, they were surprised. They didn't know anything about the AFS exchange program and wanted to know where I would stay. I explained that I would be staying with an American host family that AFS had selected, and whom I only knew from the few letters and photos we had exchanged. My classmates were incredulous. "You'll be staying a whole year with a family you don't know and eating strange American food?"

they asked. I said, "Yes! I can't wait!" They thought I was crazy. They would never leave their homes and families for a year to stay with strangers in a foreign country.

As for me, I found this trip to be such a positive opportunity; I did not understand why people thought I was crazy. I was confident that I was doing the right thing for myself. What mattered to me were my views and not the views of my friends, classmates, or even relatives.

Even though I wasn't yet seventeen, I was confident that going to America for a year would benefit me for the rest of my life. As I spent more time with the three other AFS students from Larissa, and students who had returned to Greece after their year in America with AFS, I realized that we all felt like members of a special club. The returning students were pleased about their AFS year and I saw major improvement in their language fluency.

Yes, I could not wait to be in America. In my excitement, I didn't think about how difficult the year could be or its major impact to my way of thinking and my life.

The evening before my father and I were to catch the train to Athens, several of my relatives and friends came over to our house to say goodbye. They knew I would be gone for about a year. They seemed skeptical about the wisdom of my decision but they could see how excited I was about going to America.

As I lay in my bed, close to midnight on August 5, 1971, I was thinking that the next day was going to be the beginning of a new and big chapter in my life. I tried to think of all the positive aspects of my trip. Like the excitement of flying on an airplane for the first time, which was still rare then, especially for people my age. I imagined the glamorous life of America as I had seen it in movies. I remember feeling excitement but not fear. I had eagerly anticipated my trip to America for a long time, and the next day when I woke up, I would be on my way.

My excitement was probably like my grandfather's Evangelos, when, sixty-two years earlier, at the age of eighteen, he was about to go to America, on a ship, as an immigrant. Everything about my coming to America, however, was so much easier. Not only the mode of transportation, but my knowledge of the English language, the purpose of my trip, my living arrangements, and the plan to return to Greece in less than a year. I did not see myself as an immigrant. I was a student coming for education for a limited time. I could never have guessed how this first trip would affect the rest of my life.

The Vassilis Kyriagis family in 1970. From the left, myself, my father Vassilis, my mother Maria, my sister Eleni and my brother Yiannis.

* T W E L V E *

Orientation to Kindness

I N THE AFTERNOON OF AUGUST 6, 1971, after my father and I reached Athens, we took a taxi to Athens Airport, where we met the other twenty-nine Greek AFS students. Then all the students flew together to Istanbul, Turkey, where we met more students from southeastern Europe and the Middle East.

We stayed in Istanbul overnight, and the next day we took a flight to New York. This was a chartered flight for about two hundred AFS foreign exchange students. We were a group of risk-takers and open-minded kids on a plane going to New York City with a stopover in Paris airport. We were excited about freedom and interacting with other young people from other cultures for the first time.

As soon as the plane reached cruising altitude and we were free to move about the cabin, we started making new friends. First, with whomever was sitting nearby, and later all around the plane. We were a mixed company of teenage boys and girls. The girls coming from conservative Muslim countries were free, perhaps for the first time, to talk to any boy they wanted to and did.

"Where are you from? What state are you going to?" were the first two questions in every conversation. We were from Greece, Yugoslavia, Turkey, Lebanon, Israel, Jordan, Egypt, and Tunisia, and at least of three religions—Christian, Jewish, and Muslim. But in that flight, we were all AFS brothers and sisters. We were going to different states, but we all shared the same excitement of being on an airplane, going to stay with a new family, attending a new school, and starting a new life in America. We were also teenagers with active libidos, which led to tight hugging in the aisles and heavy, high-altitude kissing, making the flight even more enjoyable and unforgettable.

After we arrived in New York, we were taken by bus to the three-hundred-acre C.W. Post University Campus on Long Island for a weeklong orientation about American life and culture. This campus, I learned later, had been built by the cereal magnate Charles William Post, and is now part of the private Long Island University.

The name of the campus and its history didn't matter to us. By the time we arrived there it was late afternoon. We were placed in our dorm rooms and had dinner. Before this, I had no idea what a college dorm was. We had no activities that evening as we were tired from the trip and went to sleep early on the narrow dorm room beds.

The next day, after a late breakfast at the sprawling campus cafeteria, we learned that there were eight dormitories that would be our home for the next six days. They housed about fifteen hundred AFS students from all over Europe, the Middle East, Africa, and South America. We were told that there was another campus near San Francisco that housed another fifteen hundred students from Asia, the Far East, Japan, Australia, and New Zealand.

The campus had large open areas with endless, well-groomed lawns, something that was new to me and I think to most of my fellow AFS students. Large, majestic oaks, elms, and maple trees offered cool shade throughout the green landscape. Comfortable wooden benches were placed under the trees and near the many flower gardens. The whole scene looked like a well-designed, well-looked-after, beautiful park, with a few brick buildings thrown in here and there, making the landscape even more picturesque. How lucky were the students who attended this university! I wished that someday I could be a student at a beautiful college campus like this.

After breakfast, we were divided into smaller groups of about fifty students and given our schedules for the week. There would be several classroom presentations each day, with time in-between for discussions and lunch, and free time for organized sports in the afternoon.

We had some personal time, around dinner, and after dinner there were parties until about ten p.m. It was a full schedule. We were told that we could explore the grounds, but not to leave the campus. Unfortunately, we did not have as much free time as I would have liked to roam and enjoy the enchanting setting.

The classes we had included topics like religion in America, politics in America, drugs and how to avoid them, living with your host family, what to do if you need to change families, high school in America, and others. We typically had either a guest speaker, a subject matter expert, or an AFS staff member speak, followed by a question-and-answer session and smaller group discussions.

On the very first day, we were also assigned and met the New York–based AFS staff member who would be our AFS advisor throughout the year. They would communicate with us via phone or mail as needed. They would write to us at least once a month to keep up with how things were going and to see if we needed any assistance in case of a problem. I don't recall the name of the young woman who was my advisor. She must have been in her late twenties, but she looked much older to me. What I recall is that she didn't like my nickname, Ben, which was given to me in Greece by my English teacher five years earlier. When she saw my real name was Evangelos, she told me that my nickname should be Vangie. This sounded like a girl's name to me. I told her that I preferred Ben, but she insisted on calling me Vangie for the rest of the week. I thought, *She can call me anything she wants, this week, but my Wisconsin host family already knows that my nickname is Ben, and I'm not going to change that.*

Some of my fellow Greek AFS students heard my advisor call me Vangie, thought it was funny, and made a point of calling me Vangie to irritate me. I ignored them, and they went back to calling me Ben.

Of all the classes we had and the subjects we discussed, the one that made the biggest impression on me and I think on many of the other students was how to answer questions that our host family and new friends would ask us about the things we saw in America.

We were patiently told that we would see and experience things that would be different from our countries, our cultures, and our religions. Perhaps some of us, in our eagerness to express our feelings truthfully, could upset our host family or our new friends. For example, they told us that we will see buildings that are different from the ones in our country, and we may be asked for our opinion about them. Some buildings might look unattractive or even ugly to us. Rather than expressing our true opinion, it would be much better to respond in a non-upsetting manner. For example, using the words "different" or "unusual" instead of "unattractive," "distasteful," or "ugly." This way we would not hurt the feelings of our hosts or friends. This was surprising to me. It sounded like AFS was asking us to disguise our true feelings or even lie.

Coming from the Greek culture, which emphasizes the expression of one's true feelings, I was confused. I remember thinking that if everyone hides their true feelings, how does anyone know when someone is telling the truth or not. Or maybe the words "different" and "unusual" are clues that the other person doesn't like something. But then, I thought, if everyone knows that "different" is just another word for "ugly" or "not attractive" why don't people just use the word that best represents their point of view or their true feelings.

This topic also generated a lot of discussion among the students. Some of us started making fun of Americans for living in constant lies, never really knowing how anyone feels about anything. Some started using "different" and "unusual" as pejorative terms in our small group discussions.

With the hindsight of my sixty-five years of age, I now understand that this was an important lesson in appreciating the skill of not hurting others' feelings. That it is better to use carefully selected words and to be sensitive toward another's point of view, their religion, their political beliefs, and their culture in general.

Perhaps this is kindness in its simplest form. It starts with practicing politeness to facilitate a positive conversation, and with the acceptance of one another's differences. It was a revelation to me to recognize that my Greek family and culture did not emphasize politeness and kindness, but the truth. We know that truth often hurts and in many cases, it hurts unnecessarily. The alternative to what we may consider truth, in our expression of opinions or feelings, is not always lies, but consideration and respect of differences.

I tried to remember this lesson when I arrived at my host family's home in Wisconsin. After a few months, when my command of the language was good enough to discuss the matter, I brought it up a couple of times in discussions as something that made a big impression on me and many other AFS students at our orientation. My host mother explained that indeed this was an important skill. I tried to remember this advice, even though at the beginning it wasn't easy. At the same time, I began to imitate my host family brothers' and sisters' speech patterns. Without realizing it, I had started to use the words "Please," "Thank you," and "That's interesting," in quantities and frequencies that were unheard of in Greece. This habit developed once I began focusing on speaking and thinking in English rather than translating my words and thoughts from Greek.

A week after my return to Greece, at the end of my AFS year, I met a group of my high-school friends at a popular outdoor café-bar in the center of Larissa. There must have been more than half a dozen of us, all done with high school, talking about many subjects, including our last school year and our summer plans. It was a long, lively, and humorous discussion. Each of us had a couple of beers and were having a good time.

Suddenly, one of my friends turned to me and said, "What is the matter with you?"

"What do you mean?" I said. "Nothing is the matter with me."

He said, "You are so goddamned polite! You're full of 'Please' and 'Thank you!' Is that the way all Americans talk?"

Everyone stopped talking for a moment and looked at me. Before I had a chance to say anything, a couple others jumped in. "Yes! That's right!" they said. Another one added, "I thought you sounded strange but could not figure out why. Now I know. You are extremely polite!"

And then it hit me. Of course, I was being polite! My year in Wisconsin had made me so. I thought that my Greek friends were right. I was being extremely polite to them, and they thought it was strange and even unpleasant! I started to laugh, because it finally dawned on me that I had absorbed the C.W. Post campus AFS orientation training, and, in that respect, I was behaving like an American! I tried to explain to them the evolution of my politeness, but they didn't want to hear it. Finally, the one who had brought it up first said, "OK, just cut this politeness crap out! We don't care about how Americans behave. You are in Greece now!" I laughed again and said, "Alright! I'll try to cut it out." But I knew that I would not cut it out.

I had recognized the impact of my Wisconsin host family acculturation and I liked the results. If I hadn't learned my lesson, I would have called my friends rude, but I respected their point of view. I knew where they were coming from, because I had been coming from the same point of view a year earlier.

The only other clear memory I have from the C.W. Post campus is the evening games we played outside our dorm, and the tall, blond, blue-eyed girls from Iceland. Among the 180 or so students living in our dorm were about a dozen girls from Iceland. They all had alabaster skin, golden hair, Aegean Sea smiling-blue eyes, sweet smiles, perfect teeth, voluptuous lips, and friendly dispositions. I thought these girls looked like ancient Greek goddesses.

During our orientation week, we had several evening music and dance events outside our dorm. A few students had guitars and played and sang mostly Beatles' and folk songs. On the first music evening, someone suggested we play the "dancing and kissing game."

We made a large dancing circle of more than fifty students, both boys and girls. One person started dancing in the center and gradually moved around the circle and finally selected a person of the opposite sex to kiss. They kissed that person on the mouth and then took their place in the circle. The kissed person went to the center and, after some dancing, kissed someone else from the circle, and so on. My goal was to kiss or get kissed by one of the beautiful girls from Iceland.

This game went on for a while, and when it got darker, the large circle of dancing students was moving in irregular form and it was hard to see who the student was who was supposed to be doing the kissing.

As a Greek proverb says, "The wolf is the happiest when there is confusion among the sheep." It soon occurred to me, and to some other boys, that the probability of getting kissed by one of the beauties from Iceland was not in our favor.

As it got darker and the circle became more irregular, I made my move. I'm not ashamed to admit that I pretended to be the person in the middle and danced my way to the places in line where the Iceland beauties were dancing. I kissed one and then moved on to the others, who were further away. I noticed that some other guys were doing the same thing. The girls must have known what was going on, as there were more guys moving inside the circle and kissing more girls, but the girls didn't protest.

The dancing and kissing game usually ended with many of the boys on a kissing spree. We were all seventeen or eighteen years old, in a beautiful spot in America, on a warm summer evening, listening to music and dancing in the land of freedom and easy love.

What is a kiss anyway? A kiss is a beautiful memory, it is a slice of life, it is freedom, it is a taste of young lust and love. For me it was also the cool taste of Iceland. It was a taste of teenage paradise that left me with an indelible, sweet, and lingering memory to this day. Thank you, beautiful girls of Iceland! I will never forget you.

* THIRTEEN *

Farm Life in America

A T THE END OF OUR week at C.W. Post campus, we were split into groups again, and the students going to the Midwest flew on a chartered flight from New York to Chicago. From there a smaller group of us boarded a chartered Greyhound bus and ended up in Madison, Wisconsin, where we spent the night. We stayed with host families, but we had no activities that evening; we were tired from traveling all day.

The next day, a small group of us, perhaps ten or so, took the regular Greyhound bus from Madison to Eau Claire. We arrived there around eight in the evening in a light rain. It was Friday, August 13, 1971, and I was happy to finally meet my American family. They were all at the Greyhound bus depot and seemed pleased to meet me. We all fit into a large red station wagon for the one-hour drive to the farm, about three miles north of the town of Barron. On the way there we talked mostly about my trip from Greece. It was still raining when we arrived at the farm around ten. We were tired and didn't stay up long.

After days of traveling, Larissa to Athens, to Istanbul, to New York City, and then a week at C.W. Post College, I was finally lying in my new bed, in the house that was to be my home for the next eleven months, with a family I had just met. As I drifted off to sleep, I felt tired but satisfied. I had arrived safely in Barron, Wisconsin. My dream of the last three years was now a reality. I was falling asleep in my new home, in America.

After my arrival in Barron, the first few days passed quickly as I got to know my new family and adjusted to daily life in my new home and the routine of the dairy farm. The 160-acre farm qualified as large by Greek standards, but by the American standards of 1971 it was considered small, and even smaller by today's standards. Howard, the father of my host family, and two part-time helpers, his sons John and Kim, milked twenty-five dairy cows. These days in Barron, the average dairy farm has about five hundred milking cows and twenty full-time workers. My host family also raised about twenty to thirty head of beef cattle, about a dozen sheep, and a couple dozen pigs.

The house was a typical medium-sized farmhouse. The first floor had a narrow entryway to the living room and formal dining room. On the other side were the kitchen and the everyday dining room. The upstairs had a bathroom and three bedrooms, one for the parents, one for my two sisters, and one for me. In the walkout basement there was a bedroom for my two brothers, a pool table, and some storage space. Across the house were the barn and a couple of equipment sheds. A vegetable and flower garden were on the west side of the yard, toward the road.

A week before school was to start, the chairperson of the local adult AFS club had a party in her home to introduce me to AFS Club members and to a few student leaders from the senior class. Everything and everyone were new to me. I didn't feel comfortable with my English or with being the center of attention, but still the party was nice. Everyone tried to make me feel welcome and gave me the impression that they understood I would need time to get settled and become more comfortable with English and with my new life. I appreciated that.

Three local boys, soon to be my classmates, came to the dinner. I was pleased with their friendliness and interest in meeting me before school started. I was impressed that all of them came separately, driving either their own or their family cars. The fact that they had driver's licenses before they were eighteen was surprising to me. Nobody I knew in Greece had a driver's license before the age of twenty-five. In 1971, in my immediate neighborhood, only two families had cars.

Everyone else went to work via bus, via bicycle, like my father, or on foot.

At the party, I struggled to figure out how to eat the fried chicken that was served, as I never had fried chicken in Greece. I watched how everyone else was eating it, and then I ended up using a combination of knife, fork, and my hands. I found the chicken tasty. Score one for American cuisine.

Speaking of American cuisine, when it comes to food, I'm not very selective and am usually willing to try just about anything. My new mother was a good cook, and I liked all the dishes she made. In Greece, we usually had meat only on Sundays, so it was a surprise to see meat on the menu every day, but I didn't mind. I enjoyed steaks and hamburgers, which were not available in Greece at the time, at least in our home.

Another surprise was to see the entire family drinking milk with every meal, the way we drank water in Greece. We only had milk for breakfast, in my Greek home. Being on a dairy farm, the family had plenty of its own fresh whole milk, which was high in butter content. I tried to drink more milk, but I could not. Soon my new mother, whose name was Marguerite but whom I called Mom, started placing a pitcher of water on the table with every meal and I usually drank water with my dinner.

The other major change was the desserts. Coming from a Greek home where we ate fresh fruit for dessert with every meal, the cookies, cakes, and other sweet desserts that my new mom made and served with lunch and dinner were foreign to me. I admit that it was not difficult to eat them, but thankfully I never got used to that. We often talked about these major differences in the diet, and I appreciated my host family's understanding. After our discussion, I felt more comfortable eating the apples and bananas that were available in the kitchen and on the dinner table and avoiding cookies and cake. However, I admit I wasn't always successful. Other that these areas, my adaptation to American cuisine was easy.

The topic of food and eating reminds me of the many long and interesting discussions my new family and I had around the dinner table. This was the time all of us gathered to share a meal and discuss the days' events and matters that came up at school or on the farm.

Most of the interesting intercultural exchanges that were part of AFS's goals took place around the dinner table. This is where I asked questions about school or American culture or talked about any problems I had. It was also where I shared things about life in Greece in general, and the specifics of my Greek family life and our city. As my English improved, our dining room discussions became more in depth, and more interesting and rewarding.

The week after the AFS party, I went to the high school with my host mother to tour the building and register for classes. My host mother was a kind and energetic woman in her early fifties, with a beautiful face, blue eyes, a quick smile, and a jovial personality. She reminded me a lot of my mother, including the extra pounds that are characteristic of many good cooks. She was a registered nurse and worked in a clinic. I never saw her do any farm-work, but I was told she used to drive one of the tractors when the boys were younger.

She seemed to know everyone at the high school, and everyone seemed pleased to see her. We first met with the school secretary, Mrs. West, who was genuinely happy to see both Marguerite and me. Mrs. West shared some brief and funny stories of the first days of previous AFS students who had spent a year at Barron. Then we met briefly with the professional and kind school principal, Mr. Schieffer, who introduced us to the tall, gregarious assistant principle, Mr. Perala. He escorted us to his office to discuss the details of my new classes. I shared with him a list of all the classes I had taken in Greece since seventh grade. He studied my list, and after quick comparisons with the Barron High School graduation credit requirements, he solemnly announced that I had enough credits to graduate without taking any more classes. That impressed my mom and me briefly, and after we shared a laugh we all agreed that I should take a typical senior load anyway. I registered for English, math, chemistry, economics, physical education, and two electives—guitar and photography.

A couple weeks after school started, Mrs. Held, the pretty, sharply dressed home economics teacher, met me in the main hallway. She introduced herself, talked about the boys' foods class she was teaching, and suggested I enroll in it. I was pleased with her initiative and personal attention and I accepted her suggestion because it sounded like an easy and fun class. I was glad that she also took care of the registration details.

School started during the last week of August. My host family and the high school principal had told me I shouldn't worry about the language issue because they thought my English-speaking ability was better than that of previous exchange students, but I worried.

After the first few days of classes, I realized that my understanding of what was said in class was not good enough. On top of that, I felt insecure about my newfound "fame." I was the only foreign exchange student in the school that year. I had never been "well known" before. Suddenly, I found myself among four hundred students who all knew who I was, while I hardly knew anyone. I sensed that everyone was judging the clothes I wore, my English accent, and my language mistakes. I felt out of place and uncomfortable.

Some of the boys engaged me in friendly conversation and I was thankful for that. Many of them wanted to know if prostitution was legal in Greece. They seemed envious when I told them that it was, and I was surprised that it was illegal in Wisconsin and almost everywhere else in the States. This was all part of the intercultural exchange process, I thought, and easy conversation.

Several students asked me about my Greek family, city, and my school in Greece, and wanted to know what I thought about Barron and the school. Others looked at me with sympathy as we sat on the heating registers in the main hallway between classes. They seemed to wonder why I put myself through this ordeal of being in a foreign country and a new school at the same time, something they probably would never do.

I imagined that most of the students, even though they knew who I was, could not care less why I was there and what my problems were. Like most teenagers, they were mostly concerned about their own problems and perhaps also preoccupied with sex.

My main worry was my lack of comprehension and fluency of the language. The inability to communicate clearly, and with ease, was a big problem. I was anxious to improve so I could understand what was being said in my classes and participate in class discussions. I worked on my homework every day and practiced my understanding of the language by watching television and asking anyone around me about words I didn't understand. It was a daily, continuous effort.

I was also eager to learn how best to interact with my teachers and classmates. In Greece, the etiquette around interacting with teachers was strict. Teachers kept their distance from the students. They were required to wear a suit and tie, and we had to address them as Mr. or Mrs. and only use their last names.

At Barron, I was surprised to see informal interactions, and even joking, between some teachers and students, and that some students even addressed the teachers by their first names.

My Greek middle and high schools, like all public schools in Greece at the time, were segregated by sex. After sixth grade, I didn't have any female classmates. In this regard, Barron High school was a much-welcomed change, but it required some adjustment on my part, which added to my anxiety. I found the girls more beautiful and more developed than the ones I knew in Greece. Their tight dresses and short pants accentuated all their curves. I was not used to interacting with girl classmates and doing that in a foreign language was even more difficult.

Speaking about clothing, during the second or third week of school, I made a big teenage fashion mistake. The previous weekend, I had purchased a new pair of white jeans and a nice reddish and white plaid shirt. I liked them very much, as they were my first American clothes and fitted me quite well. I wore them to school on Monday and got several compliments. And then I wore them again on Tuesday and Wednesday. For me, this wasn't unusual at all. I didn't have many clothes in Greece, and, like most Greek homes at the time, we had no washing machine. My mother did the laundry once a week by hand and she did not appreciate when we didn't wear our clothes for the whole week. In fact, most of my friends and classmates in Greece usually wore the same outfit the entire week.

Well, I was not in Greece anymore. I was at Barron High School, where everyone was expected to wear a different outfit every day. I was aware that all the students knew who I was, and I felt that I was being watched, but no one, up to that point, had explained to me the new outfit rule. By the third day, I sensed that something was wrong from the way some students were looking at me but wasn't sure exactly what it was. That Wednesday afternoon, when we got home from school, my sister Kathy, who was two years younger, said, "Ben, I think you may want to wear something different tomorrow because I heard some students making fun of you for wearing the same clothes for three days."

That, of course, explained the strange looks I had been getting. I thanked Kathy and we had a good discussion about how some of the students tended to be "clothes crazy," and about the gossiping that went on about what everyone else was wearing.

I understood then another aspect of "things to worry about" when attending a sex-integrated school. In my all-boys middle and high school in Greece, nobody really cared what the other students wore and how many days in a row we wore something. But when in America, you do as the Americans do. After that, I had no more teenage fashion problems.

Probably the best part of my new life was my host family. My host parents, Howard and Marguerite, whom I called Dad and Mom; my two host sisters, Teresa and Kathy; and my two host brothers, John and Kim, made me feel welcome and comfortable. John and Teresa were older and had graduated from high school and were attending community college in the neighboring city of Rice Lake. I didn't see them as much, but they were nice and helpful. Kim was in the same class as me, and Kathy was a sophomore. All three of us usually went to school together on the bus, which picked us up and dropped us off on the dirt road in front of the farm.

In my free time, I liked walking around the farm in the picturesque setting of the woods and fields, and watching the cows and sheep grazing on the gently rolling green hills. I especially liked the quietness of the farm, mixed with occasional animal sounds that made the bucolic setting even more pleasant.

The Howard Wagenbach family in 1973, my host family in Barron, Wisconsin. Front Left to Right: Kim, Teresa, Kathy, John. And back, Howard and Marguerite.

Another new and pleasant experience was the farm-work. I liked riding on the tractors and occasionally driving one while we turned and baled hay and did other farm chores.

When late September came, John and Kim introduced me to hunting, and I enjoyed walking in the woods during the beautiful fall season. Howard, John, and Kim had a big interest in guns, and they had several displayed on wooden racks on the dining room walls. This was totally unexpected and impressive as it reminded me of scenes I had seen in Westerns. Kim and John taught me about gun safety and how to use several of the guns and some pistols. Later, as an adult, I became a hunter. I still own a couple of hunting guns and have enjoyed hunting for many years.

I helped with the evening milking chores inside the barn, but I enjoyed more being out in the fields, hunting in the woods for squirrels and grouse and helping to guide the cows from the grazing fields to the barn. The vision I had had of life on an American farm, riding a horse like a cowboy and guiding a herd of cattle like in a Western, never became a reality. Instead, I walked behind twenty-five big and slow-moving cows, trying to coax them to walk a little faster to the barn to be milked, but I did not mind it.

My adjustment to my new family, to American food, and to living on the farm was easy. Life on the farm was good. My school life, however, was another matter.

* FOURTEEN *

Hard Times at Barron High School

*It is worth remembering that the time of greatest gain in terms of
wisdom and inner strength is often the time of greatest difficulty.*

Dalai Lama

AFTER ABOUT A MONTH at my new school, I evaluated
my progress. Math was not difficult because it required less
complicated language than other subjects and I had studied
it before in Greece. I had also studied chemistry before, but we didn't
have a chemistry lab in our Greek school, and I'd never done any experiments before. I liked the experiments, but not writing lab reports.

I was impressed with the extreme attention to safety by our patient
and helpful chemistry teacher, Mr. Steglich. During the labs, I was afraid
I would mishandle the chemicals and cause a fire, an explosion, or both.
Fortunately, that didn't happen. Thinking of the teamwork and fun I
had with my lab partners, LuAnn Rockman and Paula Dzubay, dressed
in our goofy-looking safety aprons and goggles, makes me smile.

My boys' foods class was the easiest and most fun of all. I could
not believe when I first walked into the classroom and saw half a dozen
complete kitchens in a row, fully equipped with ovens/ranges, refriger-
ators, sinks, small appliances, cabinets, etc. These kitchens were much
better than any of the kitchens I had seen in Greek homes.

In this class we learned to use a recipe, measure ingredients, use a
mixer and other kitchen tools, and bake. We mostly made easy desserts

and then ate what we made. The class lasted six weeks and I was sad when it was over. Thank you, Mrs. Held, for inviting me to join.

I also enjoyed my photography class very much. I'll get to that in more detail later. In my guitar class I discovered that my musical ability and talent were not zero but less than that, and I see no need to say anything more.

My English and economics classes did not go well. I struggled to understand the lectures, the assignments, and the homework. For example, in English we were studying some of the better-known Shakespeare plays. Because of my insufficient command of modern English, let alone Shakespearean English, I was mostly lost. Thankfully, the teacher occasionally used short film strips. These were rolls of 35 mm film with up to fifty images that were projected on a screen in sequential order and displayed short stories, like in a movie. Because I had never read any Shakespeare plays, these film strips usually helped me get the main idea of the story and the key plot points, but not always.

I had figured that in the death sequence at the end of *Romeo and Juliet*, a misunderstanding had caused both Romeo and Juliet to die, but I didn't know exactly what it was. I was embarrassed to ask the teacher because I was afraid the rest of the students would make fun of my questions. This and other difficulties prevented me from participating in class discussions and appreciating the story and its lessons. I did not like the feeling of being lost.

One day early in the year, in my economics class, which was taught by Mr. Ferguson, the topic of our small class discussion was education and experience. He had asked the class which one was better to have. There was silence among the ten or twelve students, which surprised me because the rest of the students didn't have my language problems. I hadn't thought about this subject before, but I knew the meaning of the two words he was asking about. I thought about them for a few moments and then raised my hand. Mr. Ferguson was pleased to see my raised hand and asked me to go ahead.

I said, "In my opinion, education is more important than experience." I stopped there, thinking that was enough.

Mr. Ferguson wanted more. He asked me to explain why I thought so and if I could give an example that would support my opinion. Well, I wasn't ready for more, because I had not thought through the subject and, anyway, I was unsure about the needed vocabulary. I said to Mr. Ferguson that I was sorry, but I was unable to explain my position further. He commended me for starting the discussion and said that I should think more about the subject, as he was sure I could support my position.

Then he turned to the rest of the class and asked if anyone agreed with my opinion. To my surprise, nobody did. Several students shared their opinions why experience was more important. Most of the students were being raised on farms, by fathers who had more farming experience than education. I supposed that most were planning to be farmers themselves, after they graduated from high school.

My Greek parents had drilled into me and my brother that education was the key to success in life, and I suspect that this had influenced my opinion that day. I thought more about what made education more important to me than experience. In my limited worldview as a seventeen-year-old, I was not able to see all the aspects of these two important variables in people's lives. I had never considered these concepts before and did not have a sufficient English vocabulary to discuss them.

When later in the class discussion Mr. Ferguson turned to me again and asked me to support my opinion, I said, "Education is more important because without it one cannot really have experience."

I did not expect that this opinion would be even more controversial than my previous one. Judging from the expression on Mr. Ferguson's face and on the faces of some of the other students, it seemed that I was now in more discussion trouble than before. What was worse, I wasn't sure if I believed what I had just said, or how to explain it further. I felt embarrassed and frustrated about my contribution to the class discussion and for my poor command of the language. I did not say anything else in the class that day.

At the end of the class, after the other students left the room, I approached Mr. Ferguson and apologized for not being able to communicate better to support my opinions. Mr. Ferguson said that it was not a problem. He was glad I had started the discussion, and my comments had encouraged the other students to participate, which was not easy for most of them to do. He assured me that I was making good progress in English and not to worry about it.

Today I may have the vocabulary skills to explain my position, but I still find the choice between education and experience difficult. It is not as simple as it may first appear. Based on my six years of university education and over forty years of work experience, my answer today would be that both are equally important. Experience can make our education more valuable and useful, and education can make experience more powerful and productive. It is always better to have both, when possible.

In all my previous school years in Greece, I had found most of my classes easy. But in Barron, I began to feel disappointed and sorry for myself. I thought perhaps I made a mistake coming to America. I had assumed that my school transition was going to be easier—perhaps not as easy as the transition from our mountain village to the city of Larissa, but certainly not as hard as it turned out to be.

I also felt isolated and had few friends. The beautiful and sexy girls that I liked were not interested in me. Perhaps my accent and the fact that I was unable to fully express myself did not help. I suppose that my lack of experience with girls was also to blame.

Speaking of beautiful girls, while I was facing adjustment difficulties in Barron, Shelley was in her small town of Amery, only thirty-one miles away, also in her senior year of high school. I've seen pictures of her as a cheerleader with long, straight, shining hair, a lovely smile, and blue eyes. Our chances of meeting then were better than zero but still low as there was no interaction between Barron and Amery high schools. A couple times in 1971, I was in a car on the way to Minneapolis, driving along Highway 46, which goes through downtown Amery. In those moments, for a few seconds, Shelley and I were about one hundred yards apart. Shelley in her house or in town somewhere, and I in a moving vehicle. Shelley has told me that it was fortunate we did not meet in our senior year of high school because we would not have had the immediate and strong connection we had when we met in Eau Claire, and she was probably right.

I kept asking my host family if my English was getting better. They assured me that it was. I asked them how long it took the other foreign exchange students to become fluent in English. They had not paid attention to that, but they told me not to worry because my English was good enough. I was doubtful.

Soon, the early winter days brought cold, snow, and more discomfort. I started to believe that it was stupid of me to have left my family in Greece, where school was easy and the weather mild, to find myself in this difficult situation, in the cold.

Then I started to miss my family. I couldn't call them, because at that time we didn't have a phone in our home in Greece. My family didn't call me because they couldn't afford the international calling rates.

My Greek friend Nick, who was with AFS in Southern California, and with whom I kept in touch via mail, wrote to me about warm, wonderful California, and how pleased he was with his life there.

The AFS advisors had warned us, in our orientation in New York, that we would probably go through this phase of feeling discouraged, and they emphasized that we had to keep busy and not think too much about our families in our home country. Each year, a few AFS students were unable to deal with the transition and asked AFS to send them back before they completed the year. I did not think that I would do that, but I started to understand why some students gave up and went back home.

I tried to keep busy and forget my difficulties, but that only worked for a while. I blamed myself for my predicament; this year in America was my idea. But I wasn't ready to admit to my Greek family, or anyone else, that I had made a mistake. This reluctance strengthened my determination to see the year through, come hell or high water. I looked in the mirror a few times and gave myself a pep talk: *Shape up, Ben, and stop feeling sorry for yourself.*

This determination carried me to the holidays. For the first time,

I celebrated Christmas and New Year's away from my Greek family. My Barron family tried to make Christmas special. We had a real tree, cut from the farm, which was a new experience for me. I helped with the lights and decorations. I received several presents, among them, a small, portable transistor radio, which was something I had wanted since I was twelve years old. But the snow and cold weather made me feel isolated. I couldn't go anywhere by myself, outside of the farm, because I couldn't drive.

I kept thinking about all the freedom I had in Greece. I could walk or take the bus to downtown Larissa to meet my friends, go to movies, or anywhere I wanted. The farm where my host family lived was over three miles away from town. There was nowhere to go in walking distance. I could do my homework, read, watch television, or play pool in the basement with John and Kim. I liked all of that. Watching television was helping me make progress with my English. But I was missing something, and I did not know exactly what it was.

This empty feeling was always in the back of my mind, making it difficult to focus on my daily activities and enjoy them. Maybe the emptiness was due to my ongoing psychological adjustments. Or perhaps I was experiencing a form of anxiety or depression for the first time in my life.

The arrival of the new year found me mostly sad, anxiously waiting for things to get better. As a New Year's resolution, I decided to try to worry less and to focus on positive things, like the good times I was having with my host family.

Looking back now, at this first Wisconsin winter of my discontent, I realize that it was inevitable. I had underestimated the difficulties of attending a new school where everything was taught in English. I also did not expect that I would miss my Greek family and friends as much as I did.

Perhaps the adjustment difficulties were meant to be part of the benefit of the AFS intercultural experience. The opportunity to see things from a totally different point of view, to deal with problems head-on and grow in the process. To learn more about your own country before you can understand and appreciate a new country and its

My Barron High School Yearbook photo, taken in August of 1971.

culture. The outcome, or takeaway of this experience, depends on how the difficulties you encounter affect you. Do they reveal your weaknesses, or help you discover your inner strength? Will you give up and decide to go back home, or deal with the difficulties head on and try to overcome them?

I believed that I would not give up, but at the same time, I was not sure how or when I would overcome my problems.

* FIFTEEN *

The Ice-Fishing Solution

JANUARY IS THE COLDEST MONTH in Wisconsin. January of 1972 looked and felt even colder to me. I never liked cold, snow or winter and all three were the worst I had ever experienced. They were not helping my other problems.

Then, on the second Sunday of 1972, early in the afternoon, Howard, our dad, came in from the barn to the living room where Kim and I were watching TV and told us to dress in our warmest clothes because we were going ice fishing. Kim immediately stood up, excited. "Alright, Ben!" he said. "This is what we've been waiting for!"

Kim and I had talked before about going ice fishing. It was one of his favorite winter activities. He was really looking forward to our first outing. I had some misgivings. I had tried to imagine standing on the frozen lake but could not. The only way to know if I would like ice fishing was to experience it. I went upstairs to my room and got dressed. I put on long underwear and jeans, two long-sleeved undershirts, a sweatshirt, and on top of all, a flannel shirt. Then I put on two pairs of thick wool socks. Most of these clothes belonged to my host brothers who were bigger. On our way out, I put on a thick stocking hat that covered my ears and heavy warm boots and grabbed a winter jacket and a pair of winter gloves.

Kim was already at the back door, dressed and smiling. "We're going to have fun, Ben," he said. "Let's go."

Before we walked outside, mom handed me a large bag. "You'll need this," she said. "It has cookies and hot chocolate. Have fun, now!" I thanked her and walked outside.

As I approached the pickup truck where Kim was headed, I saw Howard loading some large plastic pails with ice-fishing gear on the back. I could see two ice-fishing poles and several ice-fishing tip-ups sticking out of the pails. Kim had shown these to me before and explained how they work. The tip-ups are devices that suspend live bait in the water, through a hole drilled in the ice, and when a fish strikes at the bait a flag goes up as a signal to the fisherman to check the line.

I also noticed that the back of the truck was loaded with dry firewood. I assumed it was there from a farm project.

All three of us fit snugly in the cab of the pickup truck, which was a dark green Ford 1949 model. Everyone on the farm called the truck "the forty-niner," and it was Kim's favorite vehicle, as Howard allowed him to drive it to school on the days we missed the bus.

On the way to the lake, Howard asked me how I was feeling about going ice fishing.

"I'm curious to experience it," I said, "but I'm worried about the cold. It looks like a very cold day."

It was partly sunny and probably around twenty degrees Fahrenheit that afternoon with light winds. By Wisconsin standards, this was a pleasant winter day.

"Oh, don't worry about the cold," said Howard. "We'll have a very warm fire. Did you see the firewood in the back of the truck?"

"Yes," I said, "I saw it, but I didn't know that it was for a fire on the lake." After thinking for a moment, I added, "What if the fire melts the ice and we fall in?"

Kim and Howard laughed. "Don't worry about that. The fire will not melt the ice!" Howard said.

My seventeen-year-old Greek mind knew that fire melts ice. Now, instead of worrying about the cold, I started to worry about falling through the ice into the freezing cold water, and about the fact that my swimming was not that good, especially with all the heavy clothes and boots I was wearing.

Kim must have seen the worry on my face and tried to cheer me up.

"Don't worry, Ben. People have fires on the ice all the time. The ice is very thick and there is no risk of melting. You'll see. You will be warm, and it will be fun!"

I tried to imagine a big wood fire on the ice and sitting close to keep warm but the only image that came to my mind was the ice melting under my feet. I didn't say anything, and we soon changed the subject.

When we arrived at the lake, I expected that we would park and carry some of the firewood and the equipment onto the ice, not far from the truck. But the truck did not stop. Howard drove onto the ice and didn't stop until we were more than a hundred yards from the shore. Other cars and trucks were parked on the ice, too, some distance away.

The wind was stronger on the lake and it felt a lot colder as I got out of the warm cabin of the truck. We unloaded the fishing equipment, which was in three large white plastic pails, and some of the firewood, and soon Howard had a big fire going. He had built a pyramid-like structure with the largest pieces of wood at the bottom, and he used a liquid fire starter. The wood was dry, and, with the wind blowing on the lake, it didn't take long for the fire to roar and the flames to shoot up to five or six feet high. I helped Kim drill holes in the ice with an ice auger, baited the half-dozen tip-ups with live minnows, and placed them in the ice holes.

Then we returned to the fire, tipped the empty plastic pails upside-down, and used them as our chairs to sit by the fire. Howard passed around the cookies and gave us cups of hot chocolate. I felt warmer but I was still nervous about the ice melting. I positioned myself on the side of the lakeshore, in the direction where we came from, and mentally prepared myself to run for the shore at the first sign of melting ice.

I had assumed that Howard would place a piece of metal on the ice under the firewood to avoid melting, but the firewood was stacked directly on the ice. I was sure that with all the flames, and the heat of the fire, water would start pooling around the base and the fire would slowly sink into the ice. But after about ten minutes, the base of the fire looked the same as when the fire had started. There was hardly any water or other sign of melting. I was surprised, but finally I felt safe, warm, and relaxed.

I looked around me and took in the entire lake scene. It was mostly a white, empty, and peaceful landscape. There were thin gray clouds in the sky, but the sun shone through them and patches of bright blue were visible here and there. The air was crisp and clear. I smelled and heard the roaring and crackling fire.

I looked at Kim and saw happiness on his face. He was usually a worry-free, happy-go-lucky kind of guy. He was almost the same height as me, at about five feet eight, but about forty pounds heavier than my one hundred and fifty. He seemed to have a small but permanent smile on his face and a look of contentment about him. His main interests were hunting and fishing. When he was doing those activities, he was completely in his element, focused on the task at hand, full of joy and nothing else on his mind. I found that interesting and admirable because my mind was always preoccupied with so many things at the same time. I had not yet found any activity that gave me the kind of joy that Kim found in hunting and fishing.

I looked at Howard, who as usual wasn't saying much. He was in his early fifties, with a short, lean body, full of energy. He had worked outdoors his entire life, which gave him the typical sunburned farmer complexion.

Howard preferred to listen more than talk. In my first few months in Barron, I had a hard time understanding what he said because he used short phrases and expressions that sounded foreign to me. He would say things like "I recon," or "I suppose so," instead of "Yes," or "I think so." He often stopped short of finishing sentences, expecting the other person to know what he meant. It took me a few months to get used to his speech patterns and to understand him. When I finally did, I noticed that he was a good listener and paid close attention to what everyone else was saying.

As I watched Kim and Howard fishing, with the short ice-fishing poles through the two holes near the fire, I asked Howard about his memories of ice fishing as a teenage boy.

He said, "Things were much different then. Without tip-ups and the modern fishing poles. And I didn't have much free time for ice fishing."

He explained the long hours he worked on the farm, doing mostly manual labor then, and how afterwards he was too tired to do much of anything else. Back then, he didn't think ice fishing was fun. He was glad though that his sons, and now I, were able to enjoy it. He said, "it's good to get out of the house in the winter. It's better to be out in nature doing things, and not watching television."

I was listening with interest and at the same time keeping an eye on the tip-ups. When a flag went up, it meant there was action on the fishing line. Then I would shout with excitement, "Tip-up!" and Kim and I would run to see if there was a fish on the line. Most of the time it was a false alarm, as the fish would take the bait without getting caught. Then we would put on new bait and reset the tip-up.

When there was no action on the tip-ups, we sat by the fire, drank hot chocolate, and talked. Kim shared his memories of his first ice-fishing trip, when he was around twelve years old, and how much he enjoyed catching fish and just being on the lake. Howard asked me how we spent our winters in Greece, and I shared my memories of winters in the village of my youth, on Mount Olympus, with the snow, and how much we disliked winter, because of the cold and the difficulties it caused for our family and our goats and donkey.

Suddenly, I realized how immersed my mind was in this new winter activity of ice-fishing that had previously seemed so strange to me. I was sitting next to a roaring warm fire, with my American dad, Howard, and my brother, Kim, sharing stories about ice fishing, winter, and other things, as if I had done it a hundred times before. I felt that I belonged there, doing exactly that. The language was not a problem. I understood everything that was said, and I could say what I wanted without thinking about it.

Before I knew it, we had spent about two hours on the frozen lake. Toward the end, we allowed the fire to burn itself out. Howard gathered the remains and placed them in a large metal bucket. When he cleared everything, he made a point of showing me the amount of ice that had melted. There was a small indentation of less than one inch where the fire had been. The ice was more than twelve inches thick that day, so there was never any possibility of melting.

"You see?" Howard asked, "all the heat from the fire went up in the air, and not down to the ice."

"Yes," I said. "I see it now, but I would have never guessed that."

We loaded the pails with the fishing gear and everything else we had brought back on the truck and headed home as the sun begun to set. We were feeling good about the time we had spent together on the lake that afternoon. I don't recall catching any fish that were worth bringing home that day. But perhaps we captured something more valuable, about the essence of a good ice-fishing trip.

It seems to me that a good ice-fishing trip must include three ingredients: First, you must have a roaring fire to keep warm. Second, you must have homemade cookies and hot chocolate, or the drink of your choice. Third, and most important, you must have good company and good stories.

Since that day, I have gone on more ice-fishing trips. Some in ice-fishing shacks with home-like comforts. On some trips, we caught several good-sized fish. But the trip that will stay in my memory forever is this first trip, with Kim and Howard, being out on the frozen lake, sitting on the bottom side of large plastic pails, next to a roaring fire, drinking hot chocolate and sharing stories.

This trip marked a turning point in my year in Barron. It showed me a new way of looking at my language and school problems. When we went home that day, I thought more about my ice-fishing experience. At first, it had seemed to me that ice fishing should not really exist. Why put up with the cold for two or more hours when you can just stay inside your warm home? I knew that it was not just for the fish. Then it occurred to me that the long and cold winter in this part of the world was a reality they had to confront every year. Instead of trying to avoid it, the people embraced it, with hobbies like ice fishing, ice skating, snow skiing, and others. They made the choice to enjoy winter.

And then I saw ice fishing as a metaphor for my problems. I began to look at my language and school problems as my own new reality, which I needed to embrace and stop seeing as obstacles. Not only had I survived my first ice-fishing trip, but I had enjoyed it. I decided that rather than worrying about my problems, I should try to enjoy the rest of my year in Wisconsin. My classes, the language, and being away from home were not obstacles that I needed to overcome. They were new experiences that I needed to embrace and enjoy.

This turned out to be the change in my thinking and attitude that I needed. I started to relax and not worry about anything. Soon after that, out of the blue, it occurred to me that the moment I had been anxiously waiting for had already passed. I was now able to say whatever I wanted to say in my classes without any trouble and without having to translate Greek thoughts into English words. I was thinking in English. I had eagerly anticipated this moment for about six months. I had expected that there would be a single, magical moment that I would recognize as it was happening. As if I would watch a key turning, unlocking my language comprehension and fluency. The actual experience was anticlimactic; by the time I noticed the change, the key had already turned.

I started to call this change "the ice-fishing solution." The more I believed that my problems were not real, the easier they became. I noticed that I was enjoying my classes more. I was participating in discussions, joking with my classmates and even with some of my teachers. My true self, my personality, was now present, but in English.

I also discovered I was now more self-confident than ever before. I felt good that I had conquered my language and class difficulties. My classes seemed easier. Being away from my family didn't bother me anymore. I had made many friends in a new school where I hardly knew anyone when I started. My problems seemed to be solved.

I was also pleased that it became easier to talk to girls, and I went on dates with some of the girls from school that I liked. It seemed to me that I had finally reached the top of a steep hill and it was only going to be downhill for the rest of the year. And the year was going too fast. I wished I had another year to enjoy everything with my newfound attitude and confidence. The next five months were easy. I enjoyed the rest of my senior year of high school by just being myself.

Some say that you have mastered a foreign language only when you can make up jokes that are only humorous in that language. I liked jokes and I thought I had a good sense of humor. One of the things that I was surprised to learn in my first couple of months in Barron was that many jokes were told at the expense of people with Polish heritage. The assumption was that these people were slow-witted or stupid. I never learned the origin or the reasons for the jokes, but I knew it was derogatory and supposedly funny to call someone a Polack. I didn't know that I would end up using this type of humor at the wrong time and not in the best way.

Economics was a mandatory class for all seniors at Barron. The teacher, Mr. Ferguson, was known as a serious and demanding teacher, but I found him to be helpful and pleasant. The class normally met as a small group of about ten students, three times a week. Twice a month we had a large group class, of about sixty students, which was about half of the entire senior class. Mr. Ferguson had noted my language difficulties and encouraged me to participate in the small class discussions, and I appreciated his encouragement, patience, and support.

Toward the end of the year, Mr. Ferguson must have thought that my English was good enough and asked me to speak to the large group class about Greece and what I knew about the Greek economy and its relationship to other European countries. I was pleased to be asked and felt confident that I could do it, even though I was not comfortable speaking in front of groups.

As part of my preparation for the talk, I decided to project a map of Europe on an overhead slide, with all the countries' borders in black ink and the names printed inside so the students could see the geographic position of Greece in relation to the rest of Europe. Our school's audiovisual department prepared the map for me.

On the day of the presentation, after Mr. Ferguson spoke briefly to the students about some class topics, he described the subject that I was going to present, introduced me, and walked to the back of the class. I took my place behind the table with the overhead projector and looked at my classmates' faces. They were all quiet, and I guessed that they sensed I was nervous about standing in front of them. I wanted to start with something funny but didn't know what. I turned on the light of the overhead projector that had the map of Europe already on it, and then looked back to see the screen on the wall behind me, where the enlarged map projected large and clear.

I started my talk with, "Today I'm going to speak to you about the economies of Greece and Europe." As I looked at the map, I noticed the country of Poland and, without thinking, I said, "But before I start, I would like to show you Mr. Ferguson's home country," and, with my pen, I pointed to Poland on the map.

I thought this was going to be mildly funny, and it would help break the ice. Well, it did much more than that! Suddenly, a loud roar of spontaneous laughter broke out in the back of the classroom, where the boys were sitting. Loud gasps of incredulity and strange looks came from the girls in the front of the room, and I heard a loud snort from Mr. Ferguson, who was standing against the back wall.

Nobody had dared to make fun of Mr. Ferguson before in such an obvious, public way, and to his face! The boys in the back kept laughing, while I was dumbfounded. I didn't know what to do. When the laughter subsided and I had gathered my thoughts, I apologized profusely to Mr. Ferguson and tried to explain that I was trying to make a joke and that I did not mean anything bad. He asked the class to be quiet and gave me a signal to continue with my presentation.

I do not recall how the rest of the presentation was received. At the end of class, Mr. Ferguson graciously assured me that I did a good job. I apologized again, he smiled and told me to forget it.

Afterwards, my friends who had been in the class gave me mixed feedback. Some thought my joke was one of the funniest moments in their high-school years. Others told me that I had crossed the line. I wasn't sure if I should have been ashamed or pleased with myself. However, I was surprised and impressed by the way Mr. Ferguson handled this awkward incident.

Several years later, I visited Barron High School and met with Mr. Ferguson. He seemed pleased to see me and we had a long conversation about my year in Barron, and the years since then. I apologized again about my poor attempt at humor in his class, and he assured me there were no bad feelings. I am thankful for his kindness and his help and encouragement when I needed it.

The end of the school year, in June, came too soon. I earned my diploma with respectable grades. I enjoyed the formal graduation festivities and the informal, illegal drinking parties with my classmates and friends. Soon after that, the time came to say goodbye to my friends and my family and to return to Greece.

It was most difficult to say goodbye to my American family. I felt then, and even more so now, that I owe them so much for everything they did for me and for treating me like a son and a brother. I am grateful to all of them. Especially to my host brother Kim. Because we were in the same class, Kim had the burden of being my guide, my companion, my English tutor, and my closest friend. During that year and the years since, I have witnessed Kim's goodness on many occasions. I learned a lot from Kim as I watched him and his loving wife, Lynette, raise a wonderful family of two accomplished sons and seven beautiful and bright grandchildren. Kim, John, Teresa, and Kathy and my late American parents, Howard and Marguerite, will always have my love, thanks, and appreciation.

I have many wonderful memories of my year in Barron and of the many kind and helpful people I met. I wish to thank all my schoolmates, my teachers, the kind and helpful folks of the AFS Club, and everyone I met in Barron. I enjoyed the first few class reunions I attended but had to miss the recent ones because I was out of the country. I hope to attend our fiftieth reunion in 2022.

When I left Barron in June of 1972, I had no idea if I would see my American family again. I thought that perhaps I would return to Barron at some point to visit, but I wasn't sure when, if ever. Most of the foreign students of that time rarely came back to visit their host families.

I left America knowing that I was not the same person I was when I arrived. But other than my newly found self-confidence, improved English fluency, and appreciation of politeness, I wasn't sure how I had changed. I figured that I had the rest of my life to recognize the other changes. I was planning to get a university education in economics in Greece. But first I had to pass the Greek university admission tests, for which I needed to prepare as soon as I returned home.

* SIXTEEN *

The Immigrant Grandfather
Returns Home

WHEN MY MATERNAL GRANDFATHER, EVANGELOS, was admitted as an immigrant to America in 1909, he was part of the first wave of Greek immigrants. According to historians, many of these immigrants did not know whether they would ever return home. Like my grandfather, most were uneducated and had few, if any, real work-related skills. Some wanted to work for a few years, save their money, and return to their villages and retire as "rich" men.

My grandfather stayed in New York a few days and then he and two friends went by train to Chicago, where they met other Greeks from their village and nearby villages. The typical new Greek immigrants were helped by other, established Greek immigrants to find housing and jobs that didn't require knowledge of English. Jobs like dishwashers, cooks, or other menial labor jobs.

Their housing was probably a shared rented apartment in the poor section of the city, where they slept two or more to a room, sharing the rent and other living expenses. For many of these immigrants, living conditions in America were not much better than in their home villages. With the notable exception perhaps of the availability of electricity and indoor plumbing.

The following year, in the spring of 1910, Evangelos, who was nineteen years old, well-built and over six feet tall was hired to work on a railroad crew that was building a new line, from Chicago to Superior, Wisconsin.

The railroad building crews included men of several nationalities who worked together in separate teams. The Italian team spoke Italian among themselves, the Greek team spoke Greek, and so on. Each team was led by an earlier, older immigrant who spoke English and translated for his fellow workers. Often these team leaders took advantage of the new workers by withholding some of their wages as their cut for the trouble of organizing and leading the group.

The working and living conditions were terrible. Workday hours were from sunrise to sundown, seven days a week. They had to deal with heat and mosquitoes in the warm months and extreme cold in the winter, while sleeping in tents and moving almost daily as the rail lines were being laid. If they were close to a town, they could go for a bath. I've imagined warm summer days when the workers, after going many days without a real bath, would bathe in one of the many lakes or ponds of Wisconsin. It would likely be a splash bath, as I doubt many of them knew how to swim. I cannot imagine how difficult it must have been to work with metal on extremely cold days, with temperatures below zero.

The attraction of this kind of work was the higher pay and the ability to save money as the railroad supplied food and tents. Higher pay at that time was about two dollars per day. There was no union representation. The workers lived in a state of permanent fear and insecurity of losing their jobs. This was how everyone was kept in line.

By 1915, Evangelos was living and working in Duluth, Minnesota. A group of Greeks had found work and settled there after the completion of the railroad line. I learned that a group of Greek men, some of them married with children, established the Greek Orthodox Church of Duluth in 1918, with about one hundred people. This church is still in Duluth today, even though there are few descendants of the original Greeks still living there.

Winters in Duluth are colder than in most American cities. Evangelos, perhaps, had had enough of the cold and moved to Gary, Indiana in 1916, through a connection with a Greek friend, and started to work in one of the large steel mills there.

Letters to and from home took several months to arrive, and Evangelos found it hard to write long letters because he was not pleased with his job or the working conditions in general and the quality of his life in America. His work in the steel mills was difficult and dangerous. He worked twelve hours per day, six or seven days per week, in areas with extremely high temperatures and frequent work-related accidents, for about the same pay he was getting on the railroad construction crew.

In the 1910s in the United States, there were many new immigrants looking for work, and the steel mills kept wages low. There were a few attempts to establish unions, but they failed. A large steelworker strike in 1919 led to the closing of the mill in Gary, and many workers left the area to look for new jobs elsewhere. By that time, Evangelos spoke English fluently. He had attended a night school for a year and learned to read and write. He read the daily local newspaper and listened to the radio.

In 1919, Evangelos heard from a friend from his village who lived in the town of Kewanee, Illinois, about 130 miles southwest of Chicago. His friend, Yiannis Baslis, asked him to join his established business of cleaning hats and shining shoes. Evangelos took the train to Kewanee. We do not know if they had an equal shares business partnership. I do have a copy of their store stationery that reads as follows:

NEW STAR - SHOE SHINING PARLOR & HAT CLEANING SHOP
Proprietors: John Baslis and A. Matos
109 West Third Street
Kewanee Illinois
Tel: 431B

By 1920, there was growing anti-immigrant sentiment across America and particularly toward the Italians and Greeks who were the most recent European immigrants. By this time Evangelos had changed his first name to Angelo. I suspect that it was abbreviated to A. because he thought Angelo sounded too ethnic Likewise, his partner must have used the first name John because it was considered more acceptable than his Greek name, Yiannis.

It is difficult to understand that the discrimination towards the latest immigrants, from Italy and Greece, was coming from the descendants of earlier immigrants to America who had come a generation earlier, mostly from Germany and Ireland.

Kewanee, at that time, had a population of about eighteen thousand. It would be the last town where Angelo lived and worked in America. During the six years he spent there, his life and work conditions improved considerably. I had the opportunity to visit Kewanee recently and was surprised to find the original brick building from the early 1900s where his store was. The kind and helpful Kewanee Public Library staff found the home address of the business owners, in a city directory from 1922, listed as 222 North Vine street. I assumed that the original house had been replaced by a more modern one like most of the houses I had seen while driving on that street. You can imagine my surprise when I arrived at 222 North Vine street and found an all-brick built house that looked like it was built in the late 1800 or early 1900. This was the actual house where my grandfather spent the last six years of his life in America. It is a large house that probably had three or four apartments in its two stories plus a basement and some rooms in the attic. This house is approximately four hundred yards from the store where my grandfather worked so he had an easy walking commute to work.

In the early 1920s—the "roaring twenties"—the economy was booming. Practically every man was wearing a hat in those days, and there was more emphasis on men's professional appearance. Kewanee was a thriving and growing town, and their store was the only one of its kind, in a good downtown location near the train station.

Both Angelo and Yiannis worked six days a week and saved their money. In 1925 Angelo, who was thirty-four, had saved enough money and decided it was time for him to get married.

Early that year, Angelo wrote to his father that he was planning to travel to Greece to marry. His father wrote back that he had found the right girl, from a good family in the village. Her name was Katerina Kourama, she was twenty-six years old. Angelo did not know Katerina, but he remembered her older sister, who was beautiful. He wrote back to his father that if Katerina were as beautiful as her sister, he would gladly marry her. His father assured him that Katerina was just as beautiful, if not more so. In spring of 1925, Angelo left Kewanee for New York and set sail for Greece for the first time since 1909.

Back in Greece, during the years 1918 to 1922, there was another war with Bulgaria and Turkey, and the Greek economy was in tough shape. Angelo's old friend Mitros Tzatzas had become a full-time outlaw. He had graduated from petty thefts in nearby villages to bigger crimes, including kidnappings for ransom, and he had killed a man. Pursued by the police and with a price of one million drachmas on his head, he was considered one of the country's most dangerous and notorious outlaws.

When Angelo arrived in Krania, he found the living conditions there much the same as he left them, sixteen years earlier. If anything, the village looked worse to him than when he had left. There had been no improvements in the streets, the sanitation, or the general standard of living. He planned to stay about five months until the wedding, and then he and his wife would return to America.

He liked Katerina right away. She was tall, thin, with a beautiful face and long brown hair. In many ways her personality was the opposite of Angelo's. Angelo was not much for talking or laughing. He was a serious man of few words. Katerina was usually either talking or laughing and always had a story to share. She looked him straight in the eyes when she talked to him or anyone else.

Angelo told Katerina's parents that they should have the wedding in August so that in September they could leave Krania for America. Katerina had different ideas. She told Angelo that she did not want to go to America because she preferred to be close to her family, and that their village was the best place to raise a family and spend the rest of their lives.

At first, Angelo hoped that Katerina would change her mind. At the same time, his father, Giorgos, was trying to convince Angelo to stay in Greece. Giorgos said to his son, "You are marrying a nice girl from a good family. With your money from America, you can have a good life here. You have a store in America. Well, you can have a grocery store here in our village. This is the right place for you to raise a family. You are my only son and I have not seen you for sixteen years. I want to see grandchildren in this house and not die alone."

Angelo thought about this for some time. He wasn't sure what to do. At the same time, Katerina would not go anywhere with him without her parents or one of her sisters because she was afraid that Angelo would trick her by taking her on a pretend trip to Athens and from there to America. Family legend has it that it was my grandmother's stubbornness and extreme aversion to leaving her village that forced my grandfather to stay in Greece. As I thought about this major decision of his life, I had some reservations about the accuracy of this legend.

One night I found myself awake at four in the morning thinking about my grandfather's momentous decision not to return to America. It seemed to me that he probably did not take the decision lightly. Then, I remembered something my mother would say when my brother and I were teenagers and had started to dress up in adult clothes, wearing good shirts and sport coats.

We would admire ourselves in the mirror, looking all grown up, and my mother would look at us and say, "It is so important to have your family nearby to appreciate your fine-looking clothes. I remember my father telling us that one of the things he did not like about America was that he had no one there to admire his fine suits and his success. He told us that there is no pleasure in dressing up when you have no one to admire you."

I was moved by this sudden memory, and then these lyrics from the theme song of the popular 1980s TV series *Cheers* came to me:

Sometimes you want to go
Where everybody knows your name

And they're always glad you came.
You want to be where you can see
Our troubles are all the same
You want to be where everybody knows your name.

It occurred to me then that perhaps what Angelo was missing in America was the community of his people, where everybody knew his name and they were glad to see him.

When he returned to his own village, everybody knew him, and everyone noticed his fine American clothes. He probably also sensed that his fellow villagers looked up to him as a successful young man who had come from America and admired and perhaps even envied him.

I now believe that this was a major consideration in his decision to stay in Greece. Yes, his wife and father were urging him to stay. But deep inside he probably felt that he belonged in his village. That this was his home, where everyone knew everybody else.

He could not have imagined that fifty-three years later, one of his grandsons, who would have his first name, would be deciding whether to stay in America or return to Greece.

Via letters to his friend and business partner in America, Angelo arranged to sell his share in the business. By the end of 1925, his wife Katerina was pregnant, and the following year, around the time of the birth of his first child, he opened a grocery store in the village and purchased a couple of vineyards. In June of 1926, their first daughter, Maria, arrived. Twenty-eight years later, she would become my mother.

In October of 1929, the American stock market had its historic crash, followed by the Great Depression. Angelo had received a few letters from his old partner, Yiannis, but after 1930 the letters stopped coming. His relatives also never heard from him after that year, and they assumed that he had died.

When I visited Kewanee and the public library, I learned that my grandfather's business partner was married to an American lady in 1928 and the same year moved his business to a new address and expanded its operation to include clothes cleaning. He served in the US

Army for thirty months during World War II and he died in 1959, leaving behind a daughter and four grandchildren. We do not know why he stopped communication with Angelo and his family in Greece, after 1930. I wonder if his grandchildren know where their Greek grandfather came from.

When my grandfather Angelo left America in 1925, he, like all Americans, could not have known about the difficult years ahead. By deciding to stay in Greece and take his money out of America, he avoided the Great Depression, the bank failures, and the difficult times most Americans faced in the 1930s.

In 1929, Angelo was thirty-eight years old. He had been married for four years, was the father of two children, owned a grocery store and a couple of good vineyards, and was living a good life in a comfortable home in the center of the village. He was called "the American" by his fellow villagers. He was healthy and handsome, wore the best clothes in the whole village and had an attractive, thirty-year-old wife, and two children. He was one of the few immigrants from the village who had returned from America with enough money while he was still young and healthy enough to enjoy a good life.

In December of 1929, a few days before Christmas, late on a cold night, Angelo and Katerina received an unexpected visitor. When Angelo opened the door, after a loud and insistent knock, he saw a man with a full, black beard and a big smile. "Good evening, Evangelos," he said. "I heard that you returned from America and I came to see you."

Angelo had to concentrate on the visitor's face and smile for a few moments. Finally, he said, "Is that you, Mitros? I didn't recognize you with that full beard. Come on in."

It was his old friend, Mitros Tzatzas. The last time they had seen each other was twenty years earlier.

Mitros explained that night that he had come to the village to see his sick mother, whom he had not seen for a few years. He told Evangelos and Katerina about his constant moves to avoid the police. He was always worried that one of his own relatives or friends would report his location to the police.

He asked Evangelos about his years in America and how he liked his new life since his return. He seemed happy that he was doing well. He told him that he should have gone to America, too. Evangelos knew that there was a bounty on Mitros' head and advised him to surrender to the police and ask the judge for leniency.

Mitros said it was too late for that. He had killed a man and had committed other serious crimes and would be executed if he surrendered. The only choice for him was to live on the run. He always carried two guns with him and would fight the policemen if he were ever cornered. As he was leaving later that evening, after they had some wine, he told Evangelos that he was happy that they met again after all his years in America. "Enjoy your life my friend," he had said. "I hope we will meet again."

Three months later, on March 23, 1930, my grandparents heard the news that Mitros Tzatzas and two of his outlaw gang members had been ambushed by a police unit of fifteen men outside the nearby village of Elatia. An old friend of Mitros, motivated by the bounty money of one million drachmas, had reported to the police that Mitros was planning to come to the village on that day to visit friends.

The police set up an ambush outside the village, and when Mitros and his two companions appeared they started shooting. The gun battle lasted for some time. Mitros was a sharpshooter and managed to kill the leader of the police unit and one more policeman. But he was outnumbered, and the police had better positions. Mitros and his two companions were shot dead.

The battle and Mitros' death were front page news in all the Greek newspapers. Greece had been suffering from an epidemic of outlaws in the countryside. Several of them were dangerous and notorious, just like the American gangsters of the same period. The newly elected government of Greece had made it a priority to capture or kill the outlaws and had increased the resources and number of policemen dedicated to that effort. Mitros was one of the last of the well-known outlaws; his death was considered the end of that era in Greece.

For Angelo and his father, Giorgos, who was still living, Mitros Tzatzas' inglorious death was another reminder that Angelo's decision to go to America, when he did, was the right one. If he had stayed behind, perhaps he would have had the same ending as Mitros and his companions.

Giorgos shared with Angelo that it was Angelo's grandfather who had convinced Giorgos to allow him to go to America. He said, "Your grandfather was truly a wise man. He told me that I should let you go to America because he could foresee the wars coming and the future troubles of your friend Mitros. And he was right on both counts!"

By 1934, Angelo and Katerina's family had grown to five children, three daughters and two sons. By then, the Great Depression had spread worldwide, including Greece. Life in Greek cities became more difficult due to high unemployment. But life in the small village of Krania was still good. And it continued to be good for Angelo and his family until 1940. The 1940s was one of the most difficult periods in the life of the Greek people.

The last time I saw my grandfather was in late July of 1971. I was not yet seventeen years old, and I had gone to the village to say good-bye to him, because in early August, I was scheduled to go to America for my year as an exchange student. He told me he was glad that I was going. I knew that he had convinced my mother to let me go when she was adamant that I stay in Greece. My mother told me that he said to her, "Let the boy go, it will be good for him. There is not much for him here. Let the boy go!" That is all he had said to her, and it obviously had made a difference.

I thanked him for his help in changing my mother's mind, and he said, "I wanted you to go so when you return you will tell me about life in America now."

He knew that I was going to Wisconsin. He told me that he remembered spending some very cold winters there working on the railroad line and sleeping in tents. "Those nights in the tents and the early mornings of Wisconsin winter," he said, "were almost unbearable. And in the summer, the mosquitoes were insufferable. Fortunately, we were young, and we were able to survive."

As usual, he didn't talk about any of his other experiences in America. He asked me questions about the town where I was going, about my host family and my travel arrangements. As I was about to leave, he gave me a folded, crisp fifty-drachmas bill, about two dollars of that time. This was the only money and only present that I remember ever receiving directly from him. When I thanked him and told him that I would see him next year with many stories to share, I couldn't have imagined that this was the last time I would see him.

He died less than a year later, on March 17, 1972, while I was still in Wisconsin. I have few regrets or major disappointments about my life. Among those few is that due to his death, about one hundred days before I returned to Greece, I did not have a chance to talk with him about what I had seen and learned and to hear his reaction.

Now that I have reached my retirement years, I feel a closer connection with him and a deeper understanding of his character and personality, which were shaped by his sixteen difficult years as an immigrant to America. Unfortunately, he lived during difficult times, but he did well anyway. He died at eighty-one, mostly pleased with the life he had and about leaving behind five children and nine grandchildren. I am proud to have his first name and to be his grandson.

SEVENTEEN

Educated, at the University Library

FTER MY RETURN TO GREECE, in June of 1972, I started to prepare for the Greek University entrance exams. I needed to overcome two major obstacles. The first was the competition. Greece had only five universities at that time, all government owned, and tuition free. There were no private universities. The total number of places available for incoming freshmen was about eleven thousand. The total number of aspiring university freshmen in all majors was about ninety-two thousand. My chances of success were a little better than ten percent.

The second problem was that the material on which the entrance exam questions were based was from the twelfth grade of the Greek high school curriculum, which I had missed. I tried my best, but I was not surprised when my name was missing from the list of accepted students.

I announced to my parents that I was not going to take the next year's entrance exams and instead I would work and save money to attend an American university. They thought this was a good idea and they told me that they would try to help but they knew they could not afford to provide much for my tuition and related expenses. I knew their financial situation and that I could not depend on their financial assistance. I was optimistic that after I got back to America and started my studies, I would find a way to finish them.

My parents were strong believers in higher education. Even though they had been reluctant to let me go to America in my senior year of high school, they believed that studying in America was an ambitious and worthy goal that I should pursue.

In March of 1973, I took in Athens, the written and verbal tests, administered by the University of Michigan English Language Institute, and I earned the coveted Certificate of Proficiency in English. This pleased my parents as, in their mind, it justified the expenses and their worries of my year as an exchange student in America. The certificate qualified me to teach English in a private school, and I had a paid, part-time job for a six-month period doing that. Enough time to realize that I did not want to be teaching English as a profession.

During the next two years I worked as waiter, a construction worker, an office worker in a fruit processing plant. I saved most of my income, which due to unfavorable exchange rate between the Greek Drachma and the US Dollar was barely enough to cover my airplane ticket and tuition and room and board for the first semester.

Early in 1974, I applied to and was accepted by the University of Wisconsin–Eau Claire, UWEC, which is located fifty miles south of Barron. I chose Eau Claire because I wanted to be close to my AFS host family. UWEC gave me a scholarship that covered the out of state tuition, but I still had to pay the in-state tuition.

Something unexpected happened just before I was to leave Greece for America. In the summer of 1974, a general army mobilization was called to prepare for war with Turkey. The military dictatorship that ruled Greece at that time had engineered a coup in Cyprus to force unification of the island with Greece. The Cypriot population included a Turkish minority and that gave Turkey the excuse to invade and occupy almost half of Cyprus. Greece decided to close its borders and call for the mobilization of all able-bodied men, that had served in the army before, up to age thirty-five. Suddenly, the country seemed to be on a war path with Turkey.

I already had my airplane ticket and was scheduled to leave for America within a week of the mobilization, but the borders were closed, and all international flights were canceled. There was great uncertainty about everything. My brother was already in the army, serving his mandatory military service, and there was a possibility that I would be called soon because of my age. My parents were worried about having both their sons in the army while a war was coming. They told me I should leave Greece for America at the first opportunity. After about two weeks of fear and uncertainty, the borders were reopened, and international flights resumed. Fortunately, I was able to use the same ticket, rescheduled my flight, and arrived in America in mid-August of 1974.

Shortly after I left, the Greek military junta that was in control of the government resigned, and ex-Prime Minister, Constantine Karamanlis, who was in exile in France, returned to Greece to lead a new civil government. The general mobilization was called off, but the relationship between Greece and Turkey remained unstable, and the possibility of war between them continued. I did not realize then how this uncertainty and the possibility of war would help my studies.

I started my university education in the fall of 1974, as an economics major. As a foreign student, I was required to live in a dorm for the first two years. This must have been the university's way of adding some diversity to the mostly white, Midwestern student population.

My experience as a foreign student in Barron helped me adapt to the new environment. I made friends easily among the American and international students. The university had a good intramural athletics program, including a soccer league. I organized an integrated team of American and international students and we won the championship.

In my first year at the university, I was a below-average student, because studying was not my priority. I spent most of my time with friends, playing sports and going to bars. The legal drinking age in Wisconsin at that time was eighteen.

The UWEC campus was established in 1916 and is widely considered the most beautiful campus in the state of Wisconsin. It is situated on two levels, with an upper campus, on a higher plateau, where most of the dormitories are located and a lower campus, at a lower level, where most of the academic buildings are, among many trees and green open spaces. A beautiful creek and the Chippewa River flow through the lower campus.

I was finally a university student in an educational heaven, walking daily in beautiful landscapes, among thousands of beautiful girls. This campus was even more beautiful than the C.W. Post campus, on Long Island, New York and I was delighted that the wish I had had there, during my AFS orientation week, to attend a university with a beautiful campus, had come true.

I liked my classes, and the dorm living conditions and food were not bad. The only worry I had, from the beginning of my first semester, was how I would pay for the second semester.

As the first semester was about to end and registration started for second semester, I met with the international student adviser, Mrs. Rolland. I explained to her that my parents were not able to send me money due to the crisis between Greece and Turkey. This crisis was in the daily international news with wide speculation of a pending war. There were temporary bank restrictions about sending money out of the country, but it was questionable if my parents would be able to send me money without the restrictions.

Mrs. Rolland explained that there might be some university funds available for an additional scholarship, and that I should send her a formal letter requesting tuition assistance. She also explained that even though international students were not authorized to work, I should apply to the US immigration office for a work permit, based on this unexpected hardship situation in Greece. I followed her advice and sent the tuition letter and the work permit application that day.

A week later, I received a letter from the university informing me that my tuition for the next semester, and for each semester for the next three years, would be $150 instead of $650. I was so thrilled that I was literally jumping with joy! Then I realized that I still did not have the $150 for tuition nor the money for my room and the meal ticket fees. Thankfully, I was able to register by paying only fifty dollars toward my tuition, which I borrowed from a friend.

At the end of the semester, my Barron host family invited me to spend the Christmas holidays with them, until the dorms opened in January. I discussed my financial difficulties with my host mother, and she suggested I write a letter to the Barron Kiwanis club explaining my situation and asking if they could help. I did that right away. When I returned to my dorm in January, I was pleasantly surprised to find a letter from Kiwanis and a check for one hundred dollars. It came at the perfect time and enabled me to make a down payment toward my dorm room and meal ticket and to begin my second semester. The same month a letter arrived from the US immigration office in Milwaukee granting me a work permit for the entire year with an option to renew it annually.

I thought that January of 1975 was the luckiest month of my life up to that point. I didn't know at the time that it would be surpassed by next September, when I would meet Shelley.

I applied to the university bookstore and I was hired to work full-time immediately, before classes started, and twenty hours per week during the rest of the semester. My pay was $2 per hour, $40 per week, $160 per month. This meant that I would have enough income to pay for my tuition, room and board, books, and related expenses, and have a couple of extra dollars each week for a few beers, which at that time cost 25 cents a glass.

I was able to renew my work permit every year for the next three years and kept my job at the bookstore. This job plus the tuition assistance from the university made it possible for me to complete my education, and I will always be grateful for that.

Having solved my financial problems, I started to focus more on my classes and my grades. Most of my classes were interesting. Early in my second semester, in February of 1975, I discovered the source of the most enjoyable and important learning experience of my entire life—the university library browsing room.

I should have known about this room, but I had skipped the freshman tour of the library because I didn't think I needed it. What a mistake that was! One day, while I was on the second floor of the library, I noticed a friend sitting nearby reading a magazine. When I walked over and asked him what he was reading, he showed me the copy of *TIME* magazine in his hand. I looked around and noticed a large display of magazines and a rack of several newspapers. I asked my friend what this area was. He explained that it was called the browsing room and it had newspapers from the USA and other countries, and just about any magazine anyone could want.

I took my own quick tour of the browsing area, starting at the magazine display, where I saw magazines I had never seen before. *The Atlantic, Automobile, Aviation, Advertising Week, Architectural Digest, Businessweek, Fortune, Harper's, Harvard Business Review, Newsweek,* the *New Yorker, Readers' Digest*, and, of course, *TIME*, just to name a few. On the newspaper racks, I saw the local city paper, a Madison, Wisconsin paper, the *New York Times*, the *Washington Post*, the *Wall Street Journal*, a French Newspaper (*Le Figaro*, I think), a German one, a Spanish one, the *Times of London*, and others. It was amazing! I thought I was in reading paradise!

I decided right there and then that this was the room where I wanted to spend my free time. Starting that day, and practically every school day during my next three years at UWEC, the browsing room became my hangout. If I was not in class or working at the bookstore, all my friends knew where to find me.

What good fortune for me to discover that treasure trove of information and knowledge! Almost every day, especially on the cold and windy winter days in northern Wisconsin, I sat in my usual comfortable chair, getting lost in magazine and newspaper stories. I had in my hands, at one time or another, almost every magazine and newspaper in that room. And over time I gravitated toward magazines that had the most interesting stories.

I liked reading the business magazines because they provided the real-life business stories, that helped my participation in class discussions. I read the news magazines because I enjoyed keeping up with US and international news. My favorite magazines were the ones with in-depth stories by great writers, like the *New Yorker*, the *Atlantic, Harper's*, and others. I found that *The Economist* covered many important international stories not found elsewhere. When I thought I was about to run out of things to read, new issues of the magazines would magically appear on the shelves. I was simply delighted with the browsing room.

I believe that I received a solid business education through my classes at the University of Eau Claire. That education helped me greatly in my business career. In the library browsing room, I was exposed to a broad-based liberal studies education that included history, philosophy, politics, international affairs, sociology, science, and so much more.

The browsing room reading helped shape my life in a way perhaps similar to how Alexander the Great was helped by his teacher, Aristotle. Alexander said, "I am indebted to my father for my living, but to my teacher for living well." I think that for Alexander, "living well" did not mean a comfortable life. As a king, Alexander had whatever he wished for. By "living well" he meant that his teacher, through education, gave him a broader understanding of how to enjoy his life, using the tools of attention, intention, and appreciation. The browsing room gave me a similar broader understanding and appreciation. I am thankful and indebted to the university library and hope that someday I can repay that debt.

In the summer of 1975, I stayed with my host family in Barron, with free room and board, and in turn I helped with the farm chores when I was not working at my summer job at the local turkey processing plant. There I was paid $3.16 an hour, and I saved enough money that summer to pay for part of my expenses for my second year at UWEC. I was now on a clear path to enjoy and complete my university education.

* E I G H T E E N *

An American Marriage Proposal

W HEN I ARRIVED AT THE university in 1974, Shelley had already been there as a student for two years. She was in her third year and sharing a house off campus with several of her friends. As students at the same university, the probability of our meeting each other was much higher than when I drove through her town during high school. However, we were two students among ten thousand—our meeting was statistically now possible, but not necessarily inevitable. When we both signed up for the Macroeconomic Analysis class in the fall of 1975, and on the first day of the class she sat next to me and gave me that warm, radiant smile, the probability of our meeting became one hundred percent.

There is a legend that is still believed in some Greek villages today that the three Fates visit all newborn babies on the third day after their birth to confer upon them their life's destiny. This legend originated in Greek mythology where the three Fates were minor goddesses with distinct responsibilities. One held the power of life's conditions, place, and time of birth. Another held the quality of life, love, and longevity, and the third the conditions and time of the end of life.

Could the three Fates have predicted that baby Shelley, born in Amery, Wisconsin, and a young baby boy named Evangelos, born in a mountain village in Greece forty-six days after Shelley, would meet twenty-one years later at the University of Wisconsin at Eau Claire?

Science would say this is simply a matter of probability, which is rational and meaningful, but not romantic or imaginative.

After Shelley and I returned from our trip to California in January of 1976, we continued to see each other almost every day. During the summer months we stayed in Eau Claire. I had a job stocking shelves at the local Kmart store, and Shelley was working as a waitress. We had bicycles and Shelley's old but reliable Chevy Nova car.

On our free weekends we enjoyed going to a county park near Eau Claire called Big Falls. It's a beautiful spot along the Eau Claire River with a couple of waterfalls and a sandy beach. Shelley and I shared a love of nature, swimming, and picnics. It was an easy and beautiful life without schoolwork to worry about. This was about the two of us being together, out in nature, having good times.

Toward the end of the summer, we took a week's vacation together to Door County, Wisconsin. This is the peninsula that looks like a thumb in the northeast part of the state, jutting out into Lake Michigan. We went in early August and, after spending a couple nights near Sturgeon Bay, took a ferry to Washington Island and from there a smaller boat to tiny Rock Island, a state park. This park had only primitive campsites then with no services. We took a cooler with us full of food, beer, and ice, and pitched our tent right on the beach. We swam, walked on the beach and around the island, and enjoyed each other's company in tranquility, as we saw only a handful of other people there. We had warm summer weather and a relaxed and memorable vacation. When the food ran out four days later, we returned to civilization.

I had suggested Door County to Shelley because it's the only place in the Midwest that looks somewhat like the coastline of the Aegean Sea. That section of Lake Michigan is wide open and clean. Camping on the beach, on a small, quiet island, gave us the feeling that we were on an island in Greece.

I talked to Shelley often about the beauty of the Greek islands. I was familiar with Skiathos island where I had spent a whole summer when I was sixteen. We moved there for the summer because my father was on a construction crew that was building a large hotel.

Shelley appreciated my love of nature and being near water. She was an excellent swimmer, and she told me that she would very much like to see Greece and the Greek islands someday. I told her that I hoped we would do that together, and she said that she would like that very much. As for discussing our future together, that was as far as we got.

The sweet summer of 1976 went by too fast, as all good times do. Even though Shelley and I were not talking about the future, it was obvious that our first full year together had brought us closer. We were boyfriend and girlfriend, but I believe there were undercurrents of a much stronger connection which either we were not aware of or did not wish to acknowledge.

The fall semester of 1976 was Shelley's last semester at Eau Claire. She was scheduled to graduate in December, a full year and a half ahead of me, and had started to look for a job. We had no idea what the end of that semester would bring or whether we would be together afterwards, so we didn't talk about it, even though it was frequently on our minds.

Two years earlier, in August of 1974, when I was about to leave Greece to attend the university, my mother had this wish and admonition for me: "Your father and I wish you a safe trip to America and success with your studies. I ask only one thing of you—don't marry an American!" This was the same advice that my maternal grandfather had received from his grandfather before he left Greece for America. My mother knew that, and she believed that it had worked well for him.

My immediate response was, "That's the last thing you need to worry about. I promise you I will not marry an American. I do not plan to get married until I'm at least thirty. I'm going to America to get my degree and will come back as soon as I get it." That was exactly how I felt then.

During my first year with Shelley, we certainly were not thinking of marriage. We knew that her upcoming graduation would be a test of our relationship. The few times we had discussed my plans after graduation, I told Shelley that I was going to return to Greece.

I attended Shelley's graduation ceremony and was invited to join her family at a restaurant afterwards. Shelley had accepted a job as an assistant buyer at the Boston Store, which later became part of the Macy's national chain. She would be moving soon to Milwaukee, four hours away by car. Shelley's parents knew that I was leaving in a couple of days to visit Greece for the holidays. When I kissed her goodbye that day, we didn't know if or when we would ever see each other again, but I was optimistic.

By December of 1976, I had been away from my family for two and half years. My sister had just become engaged to one of my best friends, and my parents wanted me to be home for her engagement celebration, which would take place between Christmas and New Year's. My parents found the money, somehow, for the airplane ticket, and I was glad to be back home for about four weeks. It was a happy family reunion, and a wonderful holiday celebration and engagement party.

During that trip, I considered the overall state of the Greek economy, the society's organization and expectations, and found myself comparing them to the American reality I had studied and read about over the last two and half years. For the first time, the idea of returning to pursue a career and spend my life in Greece did not seem as attractive as before. Part of the reason was that when I imagined my life in Greece without Shelley by my side, it did not seem right, nor good. I was surprised that, for the first time, my calculations about my future included Shelley. This was my first inkling that perhaps living in Greece would not necessarily be the best choice for my life.

I did not mention anything to my family about my thoughts and calculations, nor to Shelley. I knew I needed more time to think about it. I showed my family a photo of Shelley and told them I had met her in a class the previous year, and that we were spending a lot of time together. My mother studied the photograph for what appeared to be a long time and told me that Shelley was a beautiful girl with a genuinely nice smile. Before she had an opportunity to say anything else, I told her that Shelley was just a girlfriend. My mother smiled and didn't say anything.

When I returned to Eau Claire in late January of 1977, Shelley had already moved to Milwaukee. I wanted to see her, so I arranged to get a ride to Milwaukee on the first weekend of the new school year. My ride dropped me off in downtown Milwaukee, not far from Shelley's office, late on a Friday afternoon. I called her from a phone booth to tell her where to meet me. She asked, "Where are you calling from?"

I told her I was calling from "a booth in the Midwest," using a line from Joan Baez's song "Diamonds and Rust." Shelley found my response clever and funny. I think it reminded her of my ability to make her laugh. From then on, "a booth in the Midwest" became my standard response when she asked where I was calling from.

Shelley's appreciation of my humor made me feel better about myself and about us being together. Our conversation flowed freely and naturally, and we were never at a loss for words, except when there was a hint about the question of our future. It was obvious that we enjoyed being together. We recognized that our relationship's future would be determined in the next few months, and we decided to let it take care of itself. In the meantime, we agreed that I would try to visit Shelley in Milwaukee every two weeks to spend the weekend together.

At that time, Shelley's younger sister, Lori, was a student at the nursing school in Eau Claire. Her husband, Randy, was working in Milwaukee, and Lori drove to Milwaukee every weekend to visit him. Every other weekend, I became one of her riders and shared the cost of gas. On these drives I was able to learn more about Shelley's family and about Lori and Randy. Gradually, a comfortable, familial relationship developed among Lori and Randy and Shelley and me.

Early in the spring semester, I had what I considered a bright idea. Rather than just being together with Shelley a couple weekends a month, why not find a way to spend the entire coming summer together? I shared with Shelley my idea and my belief that I could find a summer job in Milwaukee. If she agreed, we could live together for the summer and I would share the living expenses.

Shelley said she thought it was a wonderful idea. Then she asked, "How can a foreign student from Greece, who's attending the University at Eau Claire Wisconsin, find a summer job in Milwaukee, where he has no connections?"

I told her that although it seemed difficult, I believed I would find a job because, in this case, being Greek was an advantage. I had learned from my mother that one must use all his skills, talents, and connections to solve his problems.

I knew there was a Greek Orthodox Church in Milwaukee and I could seek connections there. The church, located in the suburb of Wauwatosa, was designed by the famous architect Frank Lloyd Wright and built in 1961. It's a major tourist attraction and is even listed in the US National Register of Historic Places.

During a weekend visit to Milwaukee in March of 1977, I called the church and made an appointment to meet with the priest on Sunday after the service. I explained to him that I was a student and needed a summer job because I was going to be staying in Milwaukee with friends and needed to save money for my next year's tuition. I asked him if he could refer me to some members of the church who might be able to give me a job or help me find one. After we briefly discussed my background and studies, he gave me the names of two men, both with Greek last names, and their phone numbers.

In the next two days, I called both men. The first wasn't planning to hire any students that summer. The second man was the late Mr. Van Liakoulis, maintenance manager for A.F. Gallun and Sons, a leather processing company. Within a week I was hired as an assistant to the plant maintenance crew, which included electricians, plumbers, carpenters, and a few laborers. The factory was located on Water Street near the Milwaukee River not far from Shelley's apartment. I rode my bicycle to work.

During that summer, because I shared in the living expenses, Shelley and I had a balanced relationship rather than one of dependency. We learned more about each other and enjoyed discovering the attractions of the east side of Milwaukee and its large, beautiful parks along the shores of Lake Michigan.

Shelley introduced me to her new friends and some of her colleagues. I thought they would look down on me because I was a foreigner and still a student. Perhaps some did. But I didn't worry about that. I believed that I was capable and had a lot of potential and didn't feel inferior to anyone. I was glad that Shelley felt the same way. I appreciated her confidence as it made me more confident in myself and in our relationship.

As the summer was coming to an end, discussions about our relationship became more frequent and more serious. Shelley was becoming anxious about what the future would bring for us. Both of us wanted to find a solution that would give us a clear roadmap for our relationship.

We found it on a Sunday afternoon in late August of 1977, just before I was to return to Eau Claire for my fall semester. I realized that I did not know how Shelley would feel about moving to Greece with me after I graduated. I had never asked her because I assumed that she would not want to leave the United States. I decided that the time had come to find out whether this could be the first step in the creation of our future roadmap.

I made Shelley an unexpected, informal, and conditional marriage proposal. I told her that I loved her and wanted to be with her. If she were willing to move to Greece with me after my graduation the following summer we could get engaged in the coming fall, get married in June of 1978, after my graduation, and move to Greece shortly after that. I had expected that this would be the beginning of a long discussion over many days, but I was wrong. Shelley's response was immediate and enthusiastic. Yes, she would gladly marry me and move to Greece with me if she would be able to visit her family in the States on a regular basis.

It was not a romantic marriage proposal, on a bended knee. It was an agreement based on Shelley's acceptance of moving to Greece to live with me, and it suddenly solved all our previous doubts and concerns. We had realized that after being together for two years, we wanted to spend the rest of our lives together, in Greece.

We were excited and happy. We decided to keep our "engagement" a secret until the late fall, when Shelley and I would visit her parents in Amery to ask them for their blessing. For all practical purposes, however, Shelley and I, after that August afternoon in Milwaukee, felt that we were already engaged to be married.

We drove to Amery in November for the weekend. Shelley's parents knew we were coming but did not know the main reason. I had met them before twice, and they knew me as Shelley's boyfriend, who was from Greece. But they had no hint what was coming, as Shelley had decided it would be better to discuss our decision and plans in person.

We arrived on a Saturday, just before lunch. After lunch, we moved to the living room, where Shelley and I sat next to each other on a sofa, her parents across from us. Shelley's father, Paul, was a dentist in his early fifties. He was an only child who had followed his father in dentistry and inherited his practice. He was intelligent and polite, had a sense of humor and conservative views. He had spent almost his entire life in Amery, a town of around two thousand people. I suspected that he wasn't sure what to think about his oldest daughter's Greek boyfriend, but the times I visited their home, he had been friendly.

Shelley's mother, Shirley, was in her late forties. She trained as a home economics teacher, but married Paul after teaching for one year in Amery. She had been a homemaker after their wedding, taking care of five children and managing the household. I knew she was smart, a good mother, a good cook, and an excellent housekeeper. It was obvious to anyone that Shelley had gotten her beauty from her mother.

I started our conversation by saying that Shelley and I had something important to discuss with them. I said, "As you know, Shelley and I have been together for two years, and after serious consideration we have recently decided to get engaged, and to marry next year, after my graduation. We would like to have your blessing."

Shelley was sitting to my left, beaming with excitement and anticipation. She looked at me smiling and then at her parents and we both waited for their response. When they heard my last two sentences, I could tell from their faces that they were surprised and trying to hide it. They seemed more disappointed than happy. They looked at each other for guidance, but neither could say anything. Then they looked at us and we didn't say anything.

Paul recovered first and asked, "What are your plans, Ben, after you graduate?"

"After my graduation, next May, Shelley and I would like to get married here in Amery, and soon after that we plan to move to Greece."

Their surprise became even bigger and more obvious. Their jaws practically dropped. They sat on their chairs looking at each other as small lines of what looked like panic appeared on their foreheads and around their eyes.

This time, Shelley's mother spoke and asked Shelley, "And how about you, Shelley? How do you feel about moving to Greece?"

Shelley could not have been more enthusiastic. "I'm really excited about it. Greece is a beautiful country, and it would be fun to live there. But we will be coming back to visit you often and you could visit us there."

To that, Shelley's parents said nothing. They seemed uncomfortable as they adjusted their positions on their chairs. They looked at us, then at each other, then back at us, and remained speechless for several moments. A long and awkward silence hung in the air. I didn't know what to do or say as I looked at Shelley and then at her parents and then back at Shelley and back at her parents and waited for a response from them.

Finally, Shirley turned to Paul, grabbed his arm, and, looking at us, said, "Could you excuse us for a moment?"

Before Shelley and I could say anything, they stood up, and Shirley led Paul by the arm through the kitchen to the lower level of their split-level house, and then to the basement.

Shelley and I just sat there looking at each other with our mouths open, perplexed. We had no idea what had just happened, and what type of discussion was going on between her parents in the basement.

I said to Shelley, "Maybe you should have told them the reason we were coming this weekend. They would have been better prepared."

Shelley said she'd thought about it but had decided it was best to do it face to face, rather than on the phone. We stayed in our positions on the sofa, in suspense, for what seemed to be a long time. Perhaps it was five or more minutes. We did not keep track and did not move.

When Shelley's parents came back, they sat in their chairs and looked at us with the most cheerful disposition they could muster, but not quite happy.

Shirley said, "Well, since you feel this is the right step for you, and you want to be together, we give you our blessing and wish you all the best!"

Everyone was suddenly relieved. Shelley rose and hugged her mother and father and thanked them. I shook hands with Shelley's father and her mother gave me a hug. Soon after that, we started to talk about the details of announcing the engagement to the rest of the family and ideas about the wedding.

From that moment on, Paul and Shirley seemed to accept me as their future son-in-law. To this day, I still do not know anything about the discussion that took place in the basement.

The week after our visit to Amery I called my parents in Greece. I had told Shelley that I dreaded that call. She knew about my mother's admonition not to marry an American.

When I called and spoke to my mother, I reminded her of the photo of Shelley that I showed her the previous Christmas, when I was in Greece. She said yes, she remembered that beautiful girl. I said, "I have decided to marry Shelley, next summer, after my graduation, and I want your blessing."

I braced myself for what I thought was coming. But it never came. She had only one question, "Are you planning to return to Greece after the wedding?"

I said, "Yes, of course."

My mother did not miss a beat! She did not say she wanted to discuss my engagement with my father. She simply said, "If you think Shelley is the right wife for you, we give you our blessing!"

Wow! is exactly what I thought. *Wow!* What a different reaction than the one I had expected! No mention of my promise three years ago not to marry an American. No crying, no private conference with my father. I always thought that my mother was a good judge of character, and perhaps the picture of Shelley told her what she needed to know. Or perhaps she trusted the judgement of her twenty-three-year-old son. Maybe the fact that we were planning to return to Greece after the wedding was enough for her. But I hoped that trust in my selection of Shelley as my wife was the main reason she accepted my decision.

Whatever her reasons were, she gave me a valuable lesson in parenthood, the lesson to trust in your adult children's judgment even when it is different than your advice to them. If she had any misgivings or reservations about my decision, she kept them to herself. The future would show whether her confidence in her son's judgement was justified or not.

A week later, our engagement announcement was placed in the *Amery Free Press*, the local newspaper. Below a photo of Shelley and me, it read:

> Dr. and Mrs. P.H. Satterlund announce the engagement of their daughter, Shelley, to Evangelos (Ben) Kyriagis of Larissa, Greece. She is an assistant buyer at the Boston Store in Milwaukee. Kyriagis is a senior at UW-Eau Claire and will be graduating in May with a bachelor's degree in Business Administration-Marketing. A summer wedding is being planned.

There was no mention that the couple were planning to live in Greece after the wedding.

* NINETEEN *

Educated, In Photography

You don't make a photograph just with a camera. You bring to the act of photography all the pictures you have seen, the books you have read, the music you have heard, the people you have loved.

Ansel Adams

DOES EVERYONE HAVE A NATURAL ability to appreciate art or even produce something of artistic value? My answer is probably yes, if given the proper exposure. The fortunate ones get the right exposure at the right times in their lives.

During my early school years, the few art classes I had left me with the impression that I was not blessed with artistic talent. However, something unexpected signaled that the art of photography might hold some promise for me.

When I was about fourteen, I lived in Larissa and walked to my English school lessons near the city center three days a week. The walk took me past a photographer's shop. I often found myself lingering at the shop's window display, looking at the photographs. Most of them were black and white wedding photographs or formal family portraits. Some of the larger photos were framed landscapes, also black and white. I was interested mainly in these landscapes, which were updated periodically. I didn't know why I was drawn to them.

Maybe because the places looked beautiful and interesting to visit. Or maybe it was the photos' unusual combinations of light and shadows.

The shop belonged to a photographer named Takis Tloupas. His photographs of landscapes and of working people were later widely distributed in books and gallery showings in Greece, and today he is considered one of the best Greek photographers of his generation. At the beginning, I had no inkling that taking photographs would be something I would want to do. But it gradually occurred to me that perhaps I could own a camera when I was older.

One day, as I looked at the photographer's display, a new photograph caught my interest. It was a color photograph of a smiling young girl, ten to twelve years old, standing in a field of wild red poppies in full bloom, holding a bouquet of poppies in one hand. In the background were a couple of dark green hills and a few white clouds, but most of the photograph was of the field of poppies and the girl. I was mesmerized by that colorful image. The bright color of the flowers, the position of the girl, the clouds and the dark hills affected me in a way no other photo had before. This is the photo that not only made me realize that I wanted to own a camera but inspired me to imagine myself taking photographs like this field of red poppies in bloom. I didn't know at the time how I would make that happen, but I knew I would try to find a way.

Three years later, in 1971, at the age of seventeen, I found myself in America, as a foreign exchange student. When I registered at the local high school at the beginning of the school year, I was pleasantly surprised to learn that I could sign up for a photography class. I registered for it right away.

As a class requirement, I had to have my own camera. With some help from my host family, I purchased a Kodak Instamatic X-15 from the local drugstore, at the price of twenty-four dollars. I still remember my excitement when I first opened the camera, put the film cartridge in it, and took my first photo, of my American brother, Kim.

I started taking photos indoors and outdoors, and I learned to work in the school's darkroom. I developed the film, cropped and enlarged the images, and printed the photos according to the class assignments.

Photography became my favorite class. I liked the teacher's lectures about composition and other techniques, the photo-taking assignments, and the darkroom work. The teacher, Mr. James Haas, had an easygoing, pleasant personality and teaching style, and was always willing to answer my questions. I learned a lot in that class and was sad when it was over. I didn't realize at the time how important that class was going to be in my future enjoyment and appreciation of photography. I am still using the skills I learned then and I am thankful to Mr. James Haas, for all that I learned in his class at just the right time in my life.

During my two years in Greece after high school and four years of college, I did not have the money or time to pursue my interest in photography. But after I graduated, in 1979, I purchased my first serious camera, the Canon AE-1 SLR, or single-lens reflex, and started to enjoy photography as a hobby. Since that time, I've taken photos around the world, in about thirty countries, with a great variety of Canon cameras and most recently with iPhone cameras.

Among the thousands of my photos are many of wild poppy fields in bloom that I took in Greece, France, and Spain. My favorite landscape photo is one of a wild poppy field near Ronda, Spain, taken in April of 2005, and it has been hanging, enlarged, and framed, in our house ever since. Nature has many beautiful faces. One of her most beguiling is a field full of wild, red poppies in bloom.

More recently, through the photography of my friend, Julie Marion Brown, an exceptional nature photographer, especially of the intricate and amazing beauty of flowers, I have discovered the micro beauty of nature which has opened a whole new world of photographic enjoyment.

What makes photography an interesting artistic endeavor? A good photograph, like all art, must tell a story or evoke emotion. If it can do both it's even better. I start with composition, unusual perspectives, and unexpected angles. I am a believer in what the late Ansel Adams said, "You don't take a photograph, you make it."

My most important tools are my experience and the skills I have slowly learned in the field. Now that I'm retired, I have the time to look at nature with more attention and intention, and to notice things I never saw before. I try to capture images that convey a story and positive feelings in a compelling way.

Over time I learned to favor three photography tools that I call the photographer's best friends. The first one is the foundation of photography, the quality of the light. After all, the word photography comes from Greek roots that mean "writing with light." The early hours of the morning and the hour around sunset are called the "golden hours," and I've learned to use them not just for sunrise and sunset photos. For many years, I concentrated mostly on the sunrises and the sunsets themselves, which I call the "main show." Often, these "main show" images can be devoid of emotion and even boring. Not long ago, I noticed that the effect or impact of the light is probably the most interesting aspect of the golden hours, and especially during the sunrises and sunsets.

Trees, grasses, wildflowers, and weeds come alive and bask in the glorious quality of the early morning light when the camera is focused on them rather than on "the show" of the rising sun. Now I usually make them my main subject, rather than the sunrise itself, even when it is over the sea. I call this approach "capturing the glow, not the show." The glow and the show together tell a more evocative story and convey that fragile, fleeting feeling of the early morning light. The same is true of the light at sunset.

My second friend are clouds and unusual weather in general. We often hear the expression, "What a perfect day! There's not a cloud in the sky." When I hear that, I say to myself, *Not for photographers!* I prefer interesting cloud formations or unusual weather. The cheerful, small, puffy clouds and the dark, large, menacing ones add interest and emotion to any landscape. In my viewfinder, an empty blue sky with no clouds is seldom worth capturing.

I have not been able to capture good images of rain. But rain is interesting because immediately after it, especially in the summer months, there are rainbows and a special sharpness in the atmosphere that produces sharp, and evocative images.

Height and a ladder are my third friend of photographers. I

discovered their importance by accident a few years ago. On a beautiful June morning, I had made a special trip to photograph the sunflower fields below our Greek village, which from above looked like bright yellow squares on a giant green chessboard. When I arrived at the first field, I realized that all I could see were the first couple rows of sunflowers, which were over eight feet tall. I had imagined images of a yellow sunflower sea in the foreground, and the green foothills of Mount Olympus and the blue sky with a few white clouds in the background. But none of that was possible with my five-foot-ten-inch height. I took a few photos, but they looked rather poor to me.

Disappointed, I start to walk to my car. Then I noticed several hay bales scattered around the field a few yards away. Something clicked in my mind and suddenly I saw the bales as the solution to my problem. I rolled five of the bales to a spot where I thought I would have the best view and then placed them in a stepped pile, two plus two plus one. The pile of hay bales was the ladder I needed to get the six feet or so of height necessary for an ideal point of view. I was excited as I climbed up. Standing in the center of the top bale, I saw the yellow sea of sunflowers laid out in front of me, as I had imagined it. I was delighted with the view and with the images I captured. Since that time, when I photograph in places where height is important for the images I want, I usually take a small folding ladder in the car with me.

Some time ago, I happened to see this quote by the late American photographer Dorothea Lange, who is considered among America's most influential documentary photographers of the Great Depression era. She said, "A camera is a tool for learning how to see without a camera." These words have special meaning for me because they helped me realize that through photography, I've learned to look at the world around me in new ways and to appreciate its beauty and magic, with or without a camera. I am grateful for that.

Considering how important and enjoyable photography has been to me over the last forty years, I was surprised a few years ago when I saw this quote by the Italian poet Camillo Sbarbaro: "The only happiness we have is the words."

My immediate reaction was that this was not true. Photographs can certainly bring us happiness, too. I decided to write a poem to refute Sbarbaro's words. As I thought more about his statement, I realized that when he used "words," he probably meant "language and stories." That changed my reaction and attitude, and a funny thing happened on the way to the poem. Instead of writing something to refute Sbarbaro's quote, I found myself writing the following:

Pictures and words

They say that a picture is a story of a thousand words.
That may be true, but in life's wars, words are the swords.

Can you take a picture of a love that is suffering alone,
or capture a destitute man's hope that is gone?
Can you photograph the love that keeps coming home,
or the hope that endures and the life that goes on?

Words paint the stories that make you and me,
and create the bonds of our humanity.

* TWENTY *

From Socrates to Steve Jobs

MY INTEREST IN PHILOSOPHY STARTED early, when I learned about the twelve gods of Mount Olympus and evolved when we studied the Greek philosophers—Socrates, Plato, and Aristotle—in high school. I talked about philosophy with Shelley often, and I must admit a tendency to overemphasize the glory of ancient Greek rationality.

Shelley must have had enough of this in our first year together, because one day she said, "Ben, you know, just because you're from Greece and studied the Greek philosophers in high school, it doesn't mean you have a monopoly on reason or truth."

Well, I did not like hearing that, but I realized she was right and afterwards I moderated my mention of philosophy and Greek rationality in our talks. My interest in philosophy, however, remained unchanged.

In the spring of 1976, I took a class called Introduction to Modern Philosophy. It was an elective and therefore it qualified to be taken without a grade, on a pass/fail basis. At Eau Claire, students could take up to eight pass/fail classes outside of their majors. If you passed, you received class credit but no grade. If you failed, you received no grade and no credit.

I liked this system because it suited my approach to education, which was to enjoy learning without the pressure of getting a good grade. I attended the classes and listened to the lectures, but I took no notes. This approach helped me enjoy the classes and I thought that I learned more.

After taking my first two pass/fail classes, I discovered that the professors usually assumed that since I was taking the class pass/fail, I wasn't as interested as the other students, and perhaps I was a "slacker." Maybe they were annoyed that I didn't take notes. Or that I asked a lot of questions, some of which were unconventional. I found their attitude and assumptions unwarranted.

When the time came for a test, I reviewed the material in the book and usually did well enough to get a C or higher if I had been part of the grading system. By the end of the semester, in most of these classes, I had developed a good relationship with the professors, who understood by then that I was indeed interested in the subject and in learning.

The modern philosophy class had about forty students, which was not conducive to class discussion. During the second week, I decided to ask the professor what I believed to be a reasonable question. I asked him if he considered himself a teacher of philosophy or a philosopher. Many students' heads turned toward me as I sat in the back of the room against the wall, and I heard what could only be described as a low-volume, collective groan.

The professor did not respond immediately. Maybe he was surprised by my question or was thinking of a proper response. Finally, he said that nobody had ever asked him that question before and he would have to answer that in the case of a teacher of philosophy the two go together. In other words, a teacher of philosophy is also a philosopher.

He seemed a little uncomfortable making this statement. Perhaps because he knew that a real philosopher would not proclaim himself to be a philosopher. I know that Socrates, for example, had never done that. He saw himself as someone who asked questions to help his students discover the truth on their own.

The professor moved quickly to another subject. To this day, I don't know why I asked him how he saw himself. Maybe I was testing him to see how he viewed his subject. I had expected he would say that he saw himself first and foremost as a teacher, which is a most honorable occupation, and one that most of the great philosophers had practiced.

I don't remember much about the actual topics of the class. The title "Modern Philosophy" now sounds generic and reminds me somewhat of the term "modern art," which some people understand to mean "anything goes." "Modern philosophy" usually refers to the philosophy developed during the seventeenth and eighteenth centuries and associated with the French philosopher Rene Descartes, who founded a philosophic movement based on reason.

What I do remember from the class is the final report that every student was required to submit before the end of the semester. Each student had to write a seven- to ten-page paper on any subject covered during the semester. By then, the professor knew that I was from Greece, that I was a business major, and that I took the class because I had a real interest in philosophy.

Unfortunately, I don't have a copy of my paper because I didn't think it was worth saving. My chosen subject was the question: How can we humans have a better understanding of our place in the universe?

I started by stating that we are taught to study history to know our past and how we have arrived to where we are today. In this case that would include both general history and the history of philosophy. The problem with studying history for answers is that it only provides information about the past, and the further back in time we go, the information becomes less complete and less reliable. I believe that it's wise and useful to study the past. But at some point, when we've gone as far back as we can, we reach a lot of dead-ends. This is also true for the history of philosophy.

There are several periods of ancient history about which we have good and reliable information. For example, the civilizations of Mesopotamia, ancient Egypt, and ancient Greece. From the Greek period, many books by historians, philosophers, and dramatists have become the foundation of Western civilization.

Imagine that we had an opportunity to speak with some of the greatest of these Greek philosophers and writers, to discuss their accomplishments and contributions and to inform them about the progress that has been made in Western civilization since their time. Philosophers like Socrates, Plato and Aristotle, or writers like Herodotus, the father of history, or Homer, the writer of the *Iliad* and the *Odyssey*. What would they think? What would they say about the current state of knowledge and our understanding of our place in the universe?

In my paper, I wrote that if we were able to have this conversation, our ancestors would be impressed by the progress humans have made in knowledge and understanding since their times. As a matter of fact, I believe that they probably would advise us not to look to the past for answers, but to the future. The past has already provided the best ideas it had. Continuous research in archaeology and related disciplines may uncover some new information, but most likely it will not be as significant as the discoveries that are being made today.

New discoveries in astronomy, biology, chemistry, physics, computer science, space exploration, and other scientific advances hold the best promise for a better understanding of our place in the universe and of ourselves. When we search for answers in the future, rather than in the past, we should have a better chance of progress and therefore a greater probability that our species will survive and thrive.

That was, in summary, the general perspective of my philosophy class paper. Looking back at it now, it seems to me that it was a rather practical and businesslike point of view, and mostly wrong.

Since that time, I have learned to appreciate that new knowledge is often a synthesis of old knowledge with new perspectives and understanding.

I had decided to major in business administration with an emphasis on marketing mostly because I thought it was a practical rather than theoretical field of study. I was attracted to the creativity inherent in marketing. I liked that there are no single, fixed answers to marketing problems. History, philosophy, and political science attracted my interest also because they deal with ways to improve humanity's quality of life both at the individual and societal levels.

The definition of "quality of life" or "the good life" is one of the oldest philosophical subjects. Some of the earliest philosophers of ancient Greece—Socrates, Plato, and Aristotle—defined "the good life" as today we would define the self-actualization stage of Maslow's hierarchy of needs. A life with knowledge, with self-esteem, significant skills, love, friendship, honor, and civic duty for our common good. For Socrates, knowledge and especially self-knowledge, to "know yourself," was the highest goal of life.

Not long ago, I discovered this quote by Bertrand Russell, the great British philosopher, mathematician, historian, and Nobel laureate:

"The good life is one inspired by love and guided by knowledge."

Russell wrote this about 2,400 years after the ancient Greek philosophers lived. It may be more eloquent and memorable than their words, but its meaning is not much different. Russell's view of the good life, in my opinion, is as concise and on target as any modern philosophy.

When my modern philosophy professor was handing out the graded papers, he called each student's name to walk up to his desk. When my name was called, before he handed me the paper, the professor looked at me with a smile and said, "This paper is much better than I expected. Too bad you're on the pass/fail system because you would have gotten a good grade."

I smiled back and said, "You know, I don't care about the grade. And I have an advantage on this subject. I come from the country that invented Western philosophy." The teacher shook his head in the affirmative a couple of times, smiled broadly, handed me the paper, and said, "Yes! You do. Yes, you do."

Twelve years later, in 1988, with the publication of Stephen Hawking's book, *A Brief History of Time*, we were able to get a new and better understanding of the creation, evolution, and history of the universe. In his last book, *Brief Answers to Big Questions*, published in 2018, Hawking presented his theory of the creation and existence of our universe that does not require a creator. A theory that when it becomes widely known and accepted, I believe will have a significant impact on our understanding and appreciation of our place in the universe.

Hawking, who was not a philosopher but an astrophysicist, is only one of the scientists whose work has advanced our understanding of the cosmos and our place in it. I believe there will be others who will continue to enhance our understanding and appreciation of the evolution of knowledge over the long history of humanity.

Nevertheless, we will probably also continue to value the thoughts and guidance of the ancient philosophers. This was made clear to me by something that Steve Jobs, the co-founder of Apple Inc., said in an article in a 2001 issue of *Newsweek*: "I would trade all of my technology for an afternoon with Socrates."

I have wondered what Socrates would say in response to such a grandiose and complimentary statement. Perhaps he would remind Steve Jobs that knowledge is the highest goal, self-knowledge the highest aspiration, and "the unexamined life is not worth living." I think that Jobs would agree with Socrates, because he often talked about similar ideas and they were reflected in his approach to life and business.

Even though a person-to-person discussion between Socrates and Steve Jobs is not possible, it seems to me that a meeting of their minds has taken place through the evolution of the technology of knowledge. I first wrote this story on an iPad tablet, which was designed and sold by Apple, a company started and greatly influenced by Steve Jobs. Arguably, Jobs and Apple have contributed to the creation of new technologies and to the dissemination of knowledge in the last thirty years, something that Socrates would approve of and appreciate.

The Politics of Rationality

M Y EARLIEST MEMORY OF POLITICS goes back to 1963, when I heard the news about President Kennedy's assassination. I was nine years old.

In the evening of November 22, I was leaving my maternal grandparents' house to go to our home. It was gray and cold when my mother, brother, sister, and I reached the street below the house. There I saw the village's only tractor stopped and the driver talking to a couple of men standing on the roadside. My mother knew that the tractor's owner had one of the two radios in the village and asked the men what the latest news was. The tractor owner said, "The news is bad! President Kennedy was killed today!"

I did not understand who President Kennedy was or why he was killed. I looked at my mother and could see that she seemed worried. At about that moment, it started to rain lightly, and looked likely to get heavier at any minute. My mother looked up at the sky quickly, gathered us three children around her, grabbed my sister's hand and mine, and said, "Let's all go home before the rain gets stronger and we get wet."

We practically ran the short distance to our house. As soon as we got inside, I asked my mother, "Who is President Kennedy? Why did they kill him and why it's bad news?"

My mother replied, "President Kennedy was an important man.

He was the president of America and now that they killed him there is a possibility of war. And if there is a new war it would be bad for everyone, including our country and our village."

I was surprised to hear this was bad for our village. I knew that America was far away. "Who killed him and why do they want to have a war?" I asked, urgently. My mother said, "I don't think the radio said who killed him. They probably don't know yet, but it must be people who want war because I heard Kennedy wanted peace."

My mother had bad memories of the war years that Greece had suffered between 1940 and 1949. Since that time, the people in our village had been working to rebuild their lives. She must have realized that her response about the Kennedy assassination worried us, and after a few moments she said, "Let´s hope that nothing bad will happen to America and to the world. There isn´t much we can do about any of that anyway."

She then reminded us that the next day was Saturday and our father was coming home from Larissa where he worked. Saturday was always a fun day in our home as our father usually brought something sweet for us, like candy or oranges, one of our favorite fruits.

In the days after the Kennedy assassination, I heard more talk about it at home, between my parents and grandparents. Our school-teacher also mentioned Kennedy on several occasions and talked about him wanting peace while other world leaders wanted war. In my nine-year-old mind, politics had to do with war and peace. I thought that my parents and other people in our village believed that they had plenty of war. They knew how bad it was and wanted no more of it. A few days later, the assassination was no longer a topic of discussion in our house and probably in the rest of the village.

When we moved to Larissa in 1964, my father purchased our first radio. We all liked listening to music in the evening. My parents also listened to the news, but I didn't pay much attention to radio news. I liked to read the news in my father´s newspaper. My father was a construction worker with a sixth-grade education. His main interests were his work and his family and home. During the week on some evenings, he went to a coffee shop frequented by construction workers and other people from our village. There he met his friends and played backgammon, a popular coffee shop game in Greece.

Every Wednesday afternoon he did the food shopping for the family. He had a bicycle he rode to work and used to carry the vegetables and fruit he purchased at the weekly farmers' market, which was held in the city center.

When I started middle school at the age of twelve, my father's newspaper, which he purchased every day on his way home from work, helped me become aware of issues affecting the entire country of Greece and the world. My parents never told us we should read the paper. At first, I started reading it out of curiosity. I read about Greek and international sports, Greek and world politics, the war in Vietnam, science, new music, the weather forecast, etc. I found the stories interesting and useful. Soon I was looking forward to the time my father would be done with the paper so I could start my reading. We had no television then as it was not available in Greece yet.

I became a daily reader of certain talented journalists called "columnists," and I could not wait to read their next column. When my father noticed that I was reading his paper after he was done, he didn't say anything, but I guessed that he was pleased. My mother complained, occasionally, that I was spending too much time reading the paper when I should be doing my homework, but I told her that I had done it already, as I usually did my homework quickly.

Perhaps I wasn't studying as much as I should have. My middle-school and high-school grades were mostly average or a little above average. I don't know if reading the paper affected my grades either way, but I found the newspaper stories more interesting than my schoolbooks.

By the time I was fifteen, I was following Greek and world politics closely and had learned something about my father's political beliefs. He was against communism and against the Greek Communist Party, which had been legalized in the 1950s. Immediately after the Greek civil war, in 1949, my father probably voted for the right-wing party as a form of resistance against communism, since he had fought against the communist insurgents from 1946 to 1949.

By the early sixties, many Greek working-class people, like my father, started to support a new party called the Center Union Party, which was moderate. This party won its first election in 1961. It tried to make some important changes, but two years later, the then-king of Greece forced the prime minister, Georgios Papandreou, to resign.

After 1963, Greece had several weak, short-lived coalition governments. Political instability and the poor economy paved the way for the military coup of 1967. Greece had to endure a military dictatorship until 1974, without freedom of speech and with the constant fear that anyone could be arrested by the police at any time.

The 1960s were a period of instability in Greece, the United States, and around the world. The war in Vietnam had serious and long-lasting repercussions not only in the US but in Greece and many other countries.

My father believed very strongly in the need for workers' unions. Even though it was not mandatory for him to be a dues-paying member of the Construction Workers Union, he joined early in his working life, paid his dues, and was an active participant in union activities.

Gradually, the union's leadership became politicized, and the communists gained the union control in Larissa and other large cities. In previous years, the Construction Workers Union waged labor fights to improve working conditions, gain health and pension benefits, etc. But after the communists gained control, it started fighting for interests that had nothing to do with construction workers. It called frequent strikes and marches to protest the American war in Vietnam.

The union demanded that the Americans stop the war and withdraw their troops. But my father was convinced that their strike would make no difference in what America would do in Vietnam. He and his construction worker friends needed the work to support their families. It was bad enough that they lost workdays due to rain or other bad weather conditions. He thought that losing paydays protesting the American war in Vietnam was stupid.

He stopped going on strike and paying his union dues and withdrew his membership. He often talked to my mother about these "stupid

Vietnam strikes!" I learned then that good people will walk away from a cause or a group whose actions no longer make sense to them.

Much later, as an adult living in the USA, I started to wonder if it is good policy for an organization to ask its members to protest something that is so far removed from their lives, with low to zero probability of success. For example, there are many worthy causes that relate to social justice that we should support. But what is the most effective way? How do you measure the effectiveness of a handful of people gathered in front of a federal building in Minneapolis, or in any other city in America, protesting a federal regulation or injustice?

Would it not be better to spend their time in more productive political activities, like organizing support for the best candidates, registering people to vote, or making sure that they and their friends vote?

Protesting and marching do bring media attention to a good cause, and that is helpful. But in the end, I believe that nothing speaks louder than the results of a local, state, or federal election. Real change, in a democracy, can only happen with real votes cast by representatives with the power to change laws or enact new ones that reflect the needs and desires of the voters. This, in my view, is real political power.

In the fall of 1981, after three years as a permanent resident, I decided to apply to become an American citizen. Even though I wasn't planning to stay in the USA for the rest of my life, I wanted the right to vote. Up to that point, I was paying taxes but had no political voice. In preparation for my citizenship test, I studied the US Constitution, the country's history, and related topics. I found my studies interesting, and they helped me pass the test easily.

On November 19, 1981, I took my citizenship oath at the Eau Claire Civic Center Inn with approximately one hundred other immigrants, most from Laos and Vietnam. The first sentence of the oath is "I hereby declare, on oath, that I absolutely and entirely renounce and abjure all allegiance and fidelity to any foreign prince, potentate, state, or sovereignty, of whom or which I have heretofore been a subject or citizen."

I had seen a copy of the oath in advance, and I was not prepared to "renounce" my "allegiance and fidelity" to Greece. I took the oath anyway because I knew that Greece would not "renounce" my citizenship.

To this day I continue to be a citizen of both Greece and the United States with current and valid passports from both countries.

Since I became a citizen, I have followed US state and federal politics closely and have voted in every election. In my first twenty years of living in Wisconsin and Minnesota, I was impressed with the American political culture. When friends in Greece would ask me what I thought was the fundamental strength of America, responsible for making it the greatest economic and military power in the world, I had a simple answer. I told them the greatest reason for America's success was its rationality. That its policies and decisions were based on facts, on research and analysis, and not on emotions and political dogma.

It is clear to me now that whenever policies are based on dogma instead of data, our democracy dies a little. I am convinced that America cannot continue to be the leading economic and military power in the world without having its economic and political decisions based on data, science, and rationality.

In my view, the goal of civilization, including our government institutions and business, is not to perpetuate the laws of the jungle. It is to make the world more humane and fairer for the greatest number of people. In the words of the late Minnesota Senator Paul Wellstone, "Politics is not about big money or power games; it's about the improvement of people's lives."

What does it take for "the improvement of people's lives?"

I believe that Bertrand Russell pointed us in the right direction when he said,

> "To live a good life in the fullest sense a man must have a good education, friends, love, children (if he desires them), a sufficient income to keep him from want and grave anxiety, good health, and work which is not uninteresting. All these things, in varying degrees, depend upon the community, and are helped or hindered by political events".

Then Russell makes the connection between the good life and the society.

"The good life must be lived in a good society and is not fully possible otherwise."

This tells me that if we want a better life, for ourselves and for everyone else, we must be working for a better society, based on democracy, justice, data, science, and rational decisions.

A Charming Relationship?

There is no more lovely, friendly, and charming relationship,
communion, or company than a good marriage.

Martin Luther

I N THE SPRING OF 1978, during my last university semester,
I was thinking about my upcoming graduation in May, my June
wedding to Shelley, and returning home to Greece. I was looking
forward to marrying Shelley but was less sure about the wisdom of
returning to Greece so soon after the wedding.

My doubts had to do first and foremost with the difficulties involved in having to serve two years in the Greek army, which was mandatory for all Greek men. I realized that it would not be easy, nor fair,
for Shelley to live alone in a new country without being able to speak
the language, while I was living on an army base with infrequent and
short furloughs. The educational deferment I had obtained was set to
expire in the summer of 1979, one year after my graduation.

I did not like the idea of serving in the Greek army. Living conditions in the barracks at that time were not what one would call state
of the art. Many barracks were in the countryside with basic housing
facilities, often without hot water or the minimum living standards of
student housing, I had become accustomed to. I thought twenty-four

months was too long, especially because the pay was barely enough to buy a pack of cigarettes a day.

The army supplied free room and board and military clothes but that was about it. I started thinking that if I could find a job, I could stay in America for a few years to get some business experience and to save money before Shelley and I returned to Greece. But I was not sure if I could find a job that suited my interests and skills.

This was my thinking in the cold month of February 1978, on my way to my eight o'clock class. The walk took me past the main university building, Schofield Hall. Outside its main entrance I saw what I knew to be graduating seniors bundled up for the cold and lined up to get in when the door opened at eight. Recruiters had started coming to campus to interview a limited number of graduating seniors on a first come, first served basis. Some seniors arrived as early as six in the morning, to sign up.

I thought that this waiting in the winter-morning cold was uncivilized at best. No job was worth standing in the cold for hours, in my opinion. I smiled as I walked by, dressed in my heavy overcoat, the black wool scarf that my mother had made, and a warm woolen hat that covered my ears. Even though it would be nice to get a job, I was not going to stand in line in the freezing cold to sign up for a job interview.

One day in late March, as the weather got warmer, I started to drop by the career office, after my morning class was done, to see if there might be any interview slots available for jobs that could be of interest to me. In the first week, the two or three times I stopped by the office I found only slots for interviews for retail management and manufacturing jobs, which were not my cup of tea. Toward the end of the second week, I saw a couple of slots for a computer sales job with Burroughs Corporation in St. Paul, Minnesota, and I signed up.

I was interested in the computer industry because then it was still young and growing and seemed to have a bright future. I knew something about Burroughs, because as part of an assignment for one of my marketing classes, I had interviewed the sales manager for IBM, in Milwaukee, and wrote a paper about its sales management practices.

At that time, IBM was the leading computer company in the US, competing with Burroughs, the second largest.

In preparation for my interview, I got a haircut suitable for the professional sales world and trimmed my full beard. The university career office and all the professors emphasized the importance of a clean-cut look, without facial hair, when interviewing for a job. I decided that a neatly trimmed beard was professional enough because I thought my facial hair made me look older and mature.

On the day of my interview, my friends and classmates saw me for the first time in my new business suit, with my short hair and trimmed beard. One of them smiled and said, "Good luck getting a sales job with a full beard."

I thought I didn't have much to lose. I could always return to Greece, with Shelley, after our wedding if I did not find a job.

Most of my classmates believed that the best approach to getting a job, besides having no facial hair, was to have as many interviews as possible, for the practice. They signed up for interviews even for jobs they had no interest in. I told them that the interviewers would figure out that they were there mostly for the practice, but they didn't care. They kept a count of the interviews they went on as a badge of honor.

My attitude was that the fewer interviews one has the better. In theory, one job interview is all that is needed if one knows what kind of job they want and is qualified for it. My friends gave me strange looks and laughed.

The day before the interview, I went to the library and read whatever material I could find about Burroughs and IBM and reread the paper I had written about IBM the previous semester. Then I felt ready. I had no idea how important that interview would turn out to be for the rest of my life.

One of the first questions I was asked by the interviewer, Jack Park, who was the Burroughs's St. Paul Branch Sales Manager was, "Why do you want to work for Burroughs?"

I was ready for this question. I talked about my interest in the computer industry and its bright future. I mentioned my paper about IBM's sales management practices and its strict and conformist approach to selecting sales representatives. I said that I didn't want to work for a company like IBM that did not allow for any individuality. Based on my reading of Burroughs history, I thought I would fit better working for Burroughs than IBM.

I could tell that Mr. Park had noticed my facial hair and the non-conformist message it conveyed. I hoped he would see the real person behind it—someone comfortable and confident about who he was. I also talked about my year as a foreign exchange student, and what I had learned about overcoming difficulties and adapting to new environments.

I could tell that he liked what he heard. He asked me if I was able to work legally in the US since I was not an American citizen. I informed him about my planned June wedding, which would qualify me to work as soon as I applied for permanent resident status, right after the wedding. At the end of the interview, he asked me if I could visit his office in St. Paul a week later to talk more about the position and meet some of his staff. I assured him I would be glad to. Even though I had no car of my own, I was sure I could find a way to get there.

The Burroughs sales position looked like a good opportunity. I was becoming more convinced that I should postpone my return to Greece and instead focus on getting a job. Shelley supported my decision and wished me good luck.

I had my second interview in St. Paul, and in the middle of April of 1978, I received an offer to join Burroughs Corporation as a sales representative with a starting salary of thirteen thousand dollars per year, plus commissions.

My university friends and classmates could not believe that I had only one job interview with one company and was offered and accepted the job. They were also amazed that I was hired for computer sales even though I had facial hair.

Perhaps they were hiding their surprise that I got the job even though I was a foreigner who spoke English with an accent. I had been concerned about this issue even though Shelley had assured me that my accent wasn't strong, and people understood me just fine.

Nonetheless, since my job was going to be in sales, I asked Mr.

Park after I received the job offer whether he thought my accent would be a problem in my dealings with clients.

He answered, "Ben, people make judgments about other people all the time. The way they look, dress, and talk. You can only influence some of these things. But not all. Your accent is part of who you are, and you cannot help that. I would not worry about it at all."

Mr. Park's answer made a big impression on me. He was my first boss, in my chosen profession, telling me not to worry about my accent, but also teaching me not to worry about things I could not change. Since that time, over forty years ago, I've never worried about speaking English with an accent. I consider my accent a natural part of who I am, and I daresay a positive one.

A week after I accepted the Burroughs job, I called my parents in Greece to inform them that Shelley and I would not be returning to Greece later that year as originally planned. I was apprehensive about the call, but also hopeful that my parents would understand.

I talked to my mother first as usual. I shared the news that I had accepted a good job with a good company and good pay. My mother was quiet for a moment, so I added, "Because of my new job, I've decided to postpone my return to get work experience and also to save money for our trip to Greece."

My mother said, "It's good you already have a job but when will you come home with Shelley? We miss you and we can't wait to meet Shelley."

I said, "Shelley and I have no money now. It will take us a couple of years to get going. We will try to come home in the spring of 1980, two years from now."

This seemed to be reasonable to my mother, and she didn't press the issue of a permanent return to Greece.

My father was more encouraging. He said, "We miss you, but you do what you need to do to start your career. We will be here waiting for you, and you can call us more often now that you have a good job." I assured him I would call often.

When Shelley told her parents that I had accepted a job in St. Paul, only one hour away from their home in Amery, and that we had decided to postpone our move to Greece for a few years, they were delighted. Shelley had been ready to move to Greece, but she was happy that we would stay close to her parents and siblings, at least for the foreseeable future.

I received my university diploma on May 20, 1978 and started my position with Burroughs on June 5. Three weeks later, on June 24, Shelley and I were married in Amery, Wisconsin.

It was a small wedding, held outdoors. We had decided that since my family could not afford to come from Greece for the wedding, the only guests were friends of the bride and groom. Shelley's family and my host family from Barron were the only other guests. About thirty-five folding chairs were set up under an oak tree in Shelley's parents' backyard. In front of the chairs, on an elevated spot in the yard, a white metallic arch was set up as the site of the wedding ceremony. Colorful flowers and white ribbons decorated the arch and flowering pots were placed around its base.

It was a hot and humid summer day as the guests arrived and took their chairs. An intriguing, faint aroma of roasted lamb spiced with garlic and oregano wafted through the air.

Shelley radiated beauty, confidence, and happiness in her white, wedding dress, like she usually did, in any kind of dress. I was proud as she held my folded arm and we walked slowly down the center aisle of the sitting guests toward the minister, who was standing underneath the arch. I was dressed in a navy-blue business suit, white shirt, and reddish tie, nervous and anxious to get the whole wedding behind me.

The minister was from the Congregational Church of Amery, and happened to be a woman, something not common at that time. A friend from college played her guitar and recorder and sang two or three songs, which Shelley and I had selected. We had written and memorized our own wedding vows. We thought that this was the least we could do as we were about to join in serious and hopefully long holy matrimony.

Shelley's parents, her four younger siblings and her two grandmothers were on the front row. Shelley's paternal grandmother, Amy Satterlund, was in her eighties with declining health, but she came wearing a long, pink dress. She was brought to the house half an hour before the other guests arrived by Shelley's father Paul, who helped her get out of the car. As Grandma Amy walked slowly, supported by Paul's arm, Shelley and I were standing a few feet away and heard her say to Paul, in her signature high-pitched voice, "Why does she have to marry a foreigner, anyway?"

Shelley looked at me and smiled. She knew I had heard her grandmother's question, and that I would not mind it. I smiled at Shelley and told her it was fine and that I was preoccupied with other, more important things. I do remember thinking, *How strange humans can be. Here was a daughter of immigrants from Norway and Sweden, a first-generation American, who had forgotten the true meaning of the word "foreigner."* I was no more a foreigner than her father was when he came to America from Norway as a young man, about one hundred years earlier. Shelley's father looked at Shelley and me embarrassed, as he tried to quiet Grandma, and led her to the house, before she could say anything else.

Immediately after the late-afternoon wedding service, the guests enjoyed a dinner of roast lamb, which had been raised on my host family's farm in Barron and supplied for the occasion as our wedding present. Kim and I roasted the lamb on a rented roasting rig and it was served with potatoes, a vegetable, Greek salad, and Greek wine. Picnic tables, borrowed from Shelley's neighbors, were placed in the backyard and set with white tablecloths and flowers for the dinner.

We had no wedding dance after the dinner, but we had the traditional cake cutting and eating ceremony and Shelley tried unsuccessfully to spread some of the cake on my bearded face. After all the guests had left, Shelley and I changed clothes, got into her car, which was already packed with our luggage, and drove to Eau Claire, where we spent our first night as a married couple, at the Holiday Inn. Just a few minutes after we left Amery, we were hit by a major rainstorm that lasted over an hour. The rain did not start until the wedding and the dinner were over and the guests had left—we interpreted that as a good omen for our marriage.

The next day we drove to Door County, where we spent a week

in a rented cabin on the shores of Lake Michigan. Like our previous trip there, we wanted to be somewhere that resembled a Greek island, which was our first choice. With our limited budget and time, Door County was as close as we could get to that. We were now Mr. and Mrs. Kyriagis, both twenty-four years old and with a combined net worth of approximately two hundred dollars, plus an old car that wasn't worth much more than that.

As I think about the wedding now, I'm sure there were some people among the guests, and even among Shelley's family, who wondered how long our marriage would last. Intercultural marriages like ours did not have a reputation for longevity. However, neither Shelley nor I had any doubt that we wanted to be together for the rest of our lives. No one thinks about marriage failure on their honeymoon.

After our week in Door County, my wife Shelley and I settled in our rented apartment in West St. Paul. This was the second month in my job in computer sales with Burroughs Corporation. My position required that we stay in St. Paul for a six-month training period, then we would move back to Eau Claire, where I would be based for the foreseeable future. Shelley took a temporary job with a leasing company as an executive assistant.

There we were, newlyweds, living in a small, one-bedroom apartment, in a new city, with new jobs and no family or friends near us. We had lived together for three months during the previous summer in Milwaukee, but that was different; I was a guest living with Shelley in her apartment. Now we had to learn how to live together as husband and wife. We both had assumed that since we had known each other for almost three years and we were in love, living together was going to be easy and wonderful. It didn't take long to realize how wrong we were.

Each of us had brought to the marriage what had been ingrained in us from a young age. This included all the images and expectations of behavior from our cultures. Shelley came from a family where the wife was the manager and main decision-maker of the household. Her mother didn't work outside the home. But Shelley grew up expecting that as a working wife she would have my help with cooking and cleaning. I, on the other hand, like my father, expected that when I came home tired from the workday, the food would be ready, and my wife would do the dishes and all the house cleaning. These expectations soon become a major source of conflict and frequent fights.

I assumed that Shelley needed to learn how to be a Greek wife. I as the husband would do the food shopping, and read the daily newspaper, just like my father. Shelley expected that the household chores would be equally shared. Instead, her husband was acting more like a master than an equal partner.

At the same time, both of us had the challenge of starting new jobs in new fields that were difficult and demanding. We both came home at the end of the day tired and stressed. Shelley didn't think it was fair for her to be doing all the household chores while I was resting or watching television. I believed that the household chores were the responsibility of the wife, and I, as the natural head of our household, deserved to be treated so.

The frequent arguments soon turned into fights that often resulted in Shelley crying and going to bed upset. We were confused, disappointed, and surprised about how unhappy we were making each other, even though we believed that we were in love. Both of us thought we were reasonable and correct in our expectations and stood our ground. After a couple months of fights, we realized we had a serious problem, and if we could not find a way to deal with it, our marriage could soon be over.

This sober realization motivated us to try harder for a while. But we could not see an easy way out of our role conflicts. I imagined how embarrassing and painful it would be if we had to end our marriage and I had to return to Greece on my own.

We continued to argue and fight, often about insignificant things like the placement of our knife block and other tools in the tiny kitchen of our small apartment. It became more like a power game and a war over who was going to give up their positions and expectations first. We were both strong-willed individuals, not willing to make any concessions.

Ben and Shelley Kyriagis, on our wedding day, June 24, 1978

As winter approached our relationship was getting worse. We both knew that we needed to change but we did not know how, or perhaps we didn't want to make the changes. This was probably the worst time of our relationship. In our three years of knowing each other, we could never have guessed we would reach such a low point. I'm sure that both of us were embarrassed to admit that we were seriously thinking of divorce only five months after our wedding. This was a terrible feeling and left a dark cloud hanging over our heads and our relationship every day.

* TWENTY-THREE *

A Lasting Solution

IN LATE DECEMBER OF 1978, as Shelley and I prepared for our move to Eau Claire, we weren't sure how we would resolve our conflicts about our new roles as husband and wife and whether or not we could save our marriage.

In Eau Claire, we had rented a house with two bedrooms, a larger living room and kitchen, and a large yard. We were pleased with our new space and hoped that as the new year was about to start, we would find a way to live together as a young married couple in love.

In my effort to come up with a solution to our conflicts, I found myself thinking about the orientation I had to American life and culture, on the C.W. Post campus when I first came as a high school exchange student. I remembered that the Greek culture's emphasis on truth over politeness was not always for the best. I realized that if I wanted a harmonious relationship with my wife, I had to change my Greek ways of thinking and acting.

I decided to take the first step in that direction and to offer Shelley a compromise. I told her that in our new home, I was prepared to accept more household responsibilities. Shelley was pleased to hear this. We had a long, sincere talk about our past fights and agreed to establish clear ground rules about shared responsibilities and boundaries. Shelley offered to do the dishes and the laundry, two jobs that I did not want to do, and in exchange I would do the chores she didn't like.

I took over almost all the grocery shopping, the garbage handling, garage cleaning, and everything outside the house, including lawn mowing and our planned vegetable garden. We decided to try to share the cooking. I had just started to do some Greek cooking because I was missing the foods I grew up with and wanted to do more of that. We felt good about our new understanding and our plan. I told Shelley that I did not expect her to become a typical Greek wife, and that we should be partners in our household and have a relationship as equals.

This was the breakthrough we needed. I apologized to Shelley for my previous attitude and behavior, and I promised to change. She welcomed my apology and my promise with tears of joy. I cannot say that I changed overnight, but as the Wisconsin winter was ending, the spring of 1979 found our relationship in a much better place, with fewer arguments and even fewer fights.

When June 24, 1979, arrived, we celebrated our first wedding anniversary with a sense of relief and accomplishment. We knew that we had averted a marriage tragedy. Our marriage had been tested, but it survived, and we now had a better understanding and appreciation of each other.

During our anniversary celebration dinner, at a fancy Eau Claire restaurant, we reflected on the fact that for most couples, the first year of marriage was usually their easiest and best. For us it was the most difficult and probably the worst. We didn't know what the future would hold, but we were optimistic that our marriage would continue to get better. This was a wonderful feeling, and something worth celebrating on our first anniversary.

In the fall of 1979, we purchased and moved into our first home in Eau Claire. It was in a great location on a quiet street, with four bedrooms and a large yard. Shortly afterwards we started making plans to take our first trip to Greece. I was excited about the trip because I had not seen my family for four years. Shelley started to worry about how she would be accepted by my family because she knew about my mother's admonition, "Don't marry an American!" from six years earlier.

As March of 1980 approached, Shelley become even more anxious about meeting her in-laws, who spoke no English—Shelley spoke only a few words of Greek. I reassured her that everything was going to be fine and there was no need to worry.

Shelley and I took three weeks' vacation, the maximum allowed by our companies, for the trip. I was not worried about whether my family would accept Shelley. I expected it to be an enjoyable trip, especially since we would be celebrating Greek Easter—the biggest annual celebration in Greece—with my family.

We arrived in Athens on March 24 after a smooth flight and spent three nights there to get some rest and to see Athens. We visited the Acropolis, the old town of Athens, and other tourist highlights of the city center. Even though I had spent most of my life in Greece, having been away for four years and showing Shelley around Athens made me feel like a tourist, in my own country.

Well rested, we boarded the afternoon train to Larissa. It was due to arrive at ten in the evening, and I had told my parents there was no need to meet us at the station as we would take a taxi home. The train was pulled by an old-style coal-burning engine that made a lot of noise, discharged a lot of thick black smoke, and moved slower than we expected. We didn't mind because we got to see some of the beautiful, mountainous countryside of Greece.

As we approached our destination, Shelley was even more nervous and anxious. We got off the train with our luggage and started to walk toward the taxi line. Suddenly, out of nowhere, my entire family appeared walking toward us. My parents, my brother, Yiannis, his wife, Vasso, my sister, Eleni, and her husband, Vassilis.

Everyone hugged Shelley and welcomed her in English and in Greek, and my brother presented her with a beautiful flower arrangement wrapped in festive colorful paper and ribbons. I saw only warm smiles, happy faces, and love and attention focused on Shelley. Her fear and anxiety suddenly disappeared, and her usual friendly and cheerful personality was on full display.

Within seconds Shelley had won everyone over. She used the few Greek words she had memorized, hugged everyone, and smiled warmly. At times like these, the eyes and the face communicate much more than any words can. It was love at first sight. My family not only accepted Shelley from that moment at the train station but showered her with love and adoration.

I almost felt that I was being ignored. But I knew it was well and good that Shelley received that warm wave of love and appreciation. From that moment on, Shelley never worried again about being accepted by her Greek family—she told me she felt loved and embraced, and I loved hearing that.

In the next few days, we stayed with my parents and received visits from all our close family relatives, my uncles, aunts, and first cousins, who wanted to meet the new American bride in the family and bring us wedding gifts.

Some of the visits were long and even difficult as I had to translate everything so Shelley could be part of the conversation, but we also had many joyful and funny moments. We enjoyed several large Greek dinners, plenty of wine, and the inevitable Greek dancing that follows Greek dinners and wine. Shelley was ready to try all the dances with joy and gusto, much to the enjoyment and endearment of our relatives. They all congratulated me for the beautiful and cheerful American bride I had married, and I beamed with pride.

Then it was time to show Shelley Krania, the mountain village where I was born and where we still had our family home, even though it hadn't been used for several years. My parents were planning to update the house to use as a summer home after my father retired. But during our visit, it was barely useable.

Shelley had heard my stories about the village where I was born and had lived my first ten years, and she was excited to be there. We decided it would be better if we went alone, just the two of us. We rented a car and drove to the village in early April, arriving at mid-morning of a sunny and warm spring day. I was twenty-six years old and had not seen the village since I was nineteen. The house of my memories was beautiful and spacious, but now it looked small, uncared for and sad.

I showed Shelley the spot near the fireplace where I was born. I had lived in that room for ten years. It looked large to me then. Now it looked tiny and not pleasant and cozy as it lived in my memories.

By 1980, most of the villagers of working age had moved to the cities, just like our family had done. There were only about one hundred people, mostly retired, still living there of the over one thousand from twenty years earlier. As Shelley and I stood on our balcony, not a single person went by on the street below our house. But in my mind's projector of my childhood memories, I saw and heard people and other village sights and sounds in full color and in stereo.

We had a picnic lunch in the yard, and afterward we went for a walk on the main street. As we walked, I shared with Shelley some of my memories of the sounds and smells of my first ten years, starting with the crowing of roosters in the early morning, the barking of dogs, the hee-hawing of donkeys, and the chatting of neighbors. The village streets of my youth were often filled with the sweet aroma of freshly baked bread or spanakopita baked in the wood-burning ovens located in every yard.

As Shelley and I approached the village park, on the north edge of the village, I stopped in the middle of a sentence. I had caught a glimpse of the wide-open vista coming into view. The wide, green valley below seemed brand new to me, as if I were seeing it for the first time. I had looked at the view through the eyes of my youth thousands of times. But I had never seen the real and complete picture until that moment.

My twenty-six years old eyes could not believe what they saw. I don't know what a religious experience feels like, as I have never had one. The feeling that I experienced that day in Krania, standing next to Shelley, was new for me. I felt my mind expanding to take in the wide and long view, all the way to the thin dark horizon line of the Aegean Sea. The coast is about eight miles away, but due to the height of our location, we saw the horizon line much further east, all the way to the Halkidiki Peninsula mountains, as far as over fifty miles away.

White houses with red-tiled roofs were sprinkled here and there in the green Pinios River valley. Mount Kissavos, on the right, rising to 6,500 feet, was dressed in its usual dark blue and green. A few small, puffy clouds moved leisurely over the pyramid-shaped summit. The beautiful scene seemed unreal to me.

I told Shelley how surprised and amazed I was that my mind was really seeing this spectacular scene as if it was the first time. Even though I had been born in the village and my eyes had taken in that view almost every day for my first ten years, its beauty had not really registered, in my mind, until I saw it again at the age of twenty-six.

Shelley was initially surprised about my excitement, but she was understanding and helpful. She sensed that I was having a positive emotional experience and was happy to share in it. I knew then, deep in my heart, for the first time in my life, that this was my true home. Where I first felt a sense of belonging and of happiness and I was moved that I was sharing this warm and special feeling with Shelley.

My experience that day is one I cannot share with my village friends and classmates who have known Krania all their lives. They haven't experienced the village with fresh eyes the way I have, and they do not have a similar reference point. It seems to me that I needed to leave Krania for several years to be able to see it clearly, the way it truly is.

Much later, when I was in my forties, I came across this quote from T.S. Eliot's poem, "Little Gidding": "We shall not cease from exploration, and the end of all our exploring will be to arrive where we started and know the place for the first time." When I read it, I felt as if it was written for me, and for my experience on that fine spring day in Krania, in April of 1980.

I treasure my village rebirth experience and the wise words of T.S. Eliot. Every time I'm back in Krania and look out at the view from the north edge of our village, I feel fortunate that I no longer take that beautiful landscape of a green valley, a mountain top, and the seacoast for granted.

TWENTY-FOUR

The Third Violin Discovery

THE STORIES ABOUT MY GRANDFATHER'S three violins were an important part of our family history and my childhood. When we moved to the city, I was exposed to many new things and new stories that moved most of our village life stories into the background, but they were not forgotten.

After Grandpa Yiannis's death in 1975, I thought we would never find out what had happened to his third violin. This saddened me because part of my grandfather's story would forever be incomplete. I couldn't imagine then that I would learn the rest of the story twenty-seven years later.

In the summer of 2002, I was in Greece and visiting my eighty-two-year-old aunt, Despina, in her village home. She spent her summers in Krania then, and the rest of her time in Larissa with her son Dimitris and his family. She was my father's only sister and my favorite aunt.

We were sitting on her balcony whose view was wide open to the green valley, Mount Kissavos, and the Aegean coast, enjoying a cold orange drink and catching up on family news and village gossip. I brought up my childhood in the village and my memories about Grandpa, including his three violins. I mentioned, incidentally, that we had never learned what had happened to his third violin and repeated for her the ditty we sang as children:

Grandpa had three violins.
The first one was smashed to pieces by Grandma.
The second one was stolen by a German soldier.
Nobody knows what has happened to his third violin.

My aunt smiled and said, "I know what happened to the third violin!" I almost jumped up from my chair and spilled my drink on my lap. I took a couple deep breaths, sat at the edge of my chair, and leaned in.

"You do?" I asked, eagerly. "Our grandpa always told us he did not remember!"

"Well," my aunt said, with a smile, "I am sure he remembered! He just didn't want to talk about it."

I was amazed and could not say anything. I leaned in more closely, with my eyes wide open and my mouth half opened. My aunt smiled again—she must have understood how anxious I was to hear her story, so she took a deep breath and continued:

"It happened a couple of weeks before my wedding, in the fall of 1948. Our wedding was at a time that the family finances were really poor. Your grandpa was not working. Your father was in the army and, even though we had a small wedding, we needed money to buy my wedding dress and to pay for food for the guests. The only thing of value your grandpa had was his violin. He didn't want to borrow money for his only daughter's wedding. He was too proud for that. So, he secretly went to the village of Rapsani, on foot, and sold his violin to a friend of his who had wanted it.

He didn't tell anyone about it. Not even your grandma. I had assumed that he had borrowed the money for the wedding from a friend or a relative. I learned about the violin sale a year later, when I was told by a friend of a friend that her father had purchased a violin from someone in Krania. The only person in Krania who had a violin was your grandfather."

My aunt stopped, took another deep breath, and grinned. I guessed that she was enjoying seeing the surprise on my face. Then she said, "Well, now you know what happened to Grandpa's third violin."

I sat there speechless, something that hardly ever happens. This was not the behavior I had expected from my grandfather. It was not in his character, at least as I knew him. It had seemed more likely to me that he would borrow the money rather than sell his violin, but he did not. Suddenly I understood his reluctance, over many years and our many questions, to talk about his third violin. It all made sense.

My grandpa, Yiannis, had sold the most personal and valuable thing he owned, his violin, so that his daughter could have a decent wedding. He did not want to borrow money for such an important event in his only daughter's life. He was too proud for that, and he did a difficult and honorable thing for his family.

I sat there quietly for a minute, thinking about his sacrifice. Then I thanked my aunt and told her how impressed I was with Grandpa's behavior and how pleased I was that I finally knew the fate of his third and last violin. She grinned, satisfied that she had provided the answer to my forty-year-old question.

Now that we know what happened to Grandpa's third violin, the ditty needs to be revised:

Grandpa had three violins.
The first one was smashed to pieces by Grandma.
The second one was stolen by a German soldier.
And he used his third violin to preserve his family's honor and
good name.

I have shared my grandfather's life through the stories of his three violins to highlight his unique talent as a self-taught player, his difficult and interesting life, and his character during an important time for his daughter and a moment when his family's honor was at stake. His life was more complicated than his experience as a violin player.

Having reached the age of sixty-five myself, I now see my grandfather's behavior differently. I suspect that losing both his parents at the age of twelve had most likely affected greatly his personality and the rest of his life. Did he receive enough affection and attention in his early years? Was his need for attention as the life of any party a result of what he had lost when he was young?

Considering all his difficulties in his formative years, my grandfather did OK. He was an honorable man. He was well liked by his friends and by the people who knew him. He had a talent for music and storytelling, and he had two well-adjusted and accomplished children and six grandchildren.

He was not a financially successful man, but at a difficult time, when he had to preserve his family's honor and good name, he sacrificed the most valuable and dearest thing to him, his violin.

This unexpected turn in the story of Grandpa's three violins reminds me of his favorite war story, which we heard many times and never tired of.

During the Balkan War of 1913, while Grandpa was in the army, Greece was fighting with Bulgaria in what today is northeastern Greece. During a battle, Grandpa was cut off from the rest of his unit, in the front. He was lost in a wooded area and could not find his way back to his unit. Soon it got dark, and he was forced to spend the night where he was.

He found a ditch covered with bushes and slept there. It was early summer, and warm enough. When morning came, he didn't know what to do. He had no food, little water, and few bullets left for his weapon. He had no idea where or how far away his unit was or how close he was to the Bulgarian army line.

Suddenly, he heard people speaking Bulgarian nearby but couldn't see anyone, so he fired his remaining bullets in the direction of the voices. When he realized that he had fired his last bullet, he stayed in his hiding place, hoping that his unit heard the shots and would come to the area soon. He feared that if the Bulgarian soldiers arrived first, he would have to surrender.

Around noon, he heard more Bulgarian voices near his hiding place and saw two Bulgarian soldiers walking without weapons and with their hands up. One was holding in one hand a makeshift white flag that looked like a handkerchief to Grandpa. After they passed by his hiding place, without seeing him, Grandpa jumped up behind them and aimed his empty weapon at them. With hand gestures and the few Bulgarian words, he knew, directed them to keep walking with their hands up. It soon appeared that the Bulgarian soldiers knew where the Greek army front line was, and they were walking in that direction.

As they approached the line of Grandpa's army unit, his fellow Greek soldiers recognized him, started to whistle and cheer, and welcomed Grandpa as a hero. They told him they thought he was either dead or taken prisoner by the Bulgarians and were glad and impressed that he was alive and bringing back Bulgarian prisoners. Grandpa received a commendation from his superiors and was treated to a special meal and some well-needed rest.

In his telling of the story, Grandpa would always pause here for a few moments. Then he would look at his audience with a mischievous smile and say, "Of course, I never mentioned to anyone that I was completely out of ammunition and was prepared to surrender myself before the two Bulgarians showed up with their hands up. I guess the firing of my last bullets scared them to surrender!"

This story reminds me of how Grandpa could make the best out of a difficult and risky situation and how he saw the humorous side of it, even when his life was in danger.

I believe he was a good man who lived during difficult times as well as he could with what he had, which is no small accomplishment. I'm glad to have known him and proud to be his grandson.

TWENTY-FIVE

Growing an International Business

Being in business is not about making money. It is a way to become who you are.

Paul Hawken, *Growing a Business*

WHEN I WAS ABOUT TWELVE or thirteen years old, I declared to my family and friends that my future profession was going to be teacher. I was probably influenced by a couple of Greek movies I had seen that had likable teacher characters. I wanted to be an elementary teacher because they seemed to be able to influence young minds.

Later, in high school, I thought that a military officer would be a better profession. I was attracted by the power to give orders to soldiers under my command.

After my senior year as an exchange student in America, I decided that economics was a more suitable field of study and career for me. It offered the potential of understanding how a country's economy worked. I had a vague idea that perhaps I would work in a bank or for a large business, in a management position.

When I enrolled at the University of Wisconsin in Eau Claire, in the fall of 1974, my intended major was economics. In the spring semester of my third year, in 1977, I took a marketing class called "Promotion." The professor was Dr. William J. Hannaford, who was in his early thirties and had started teaching at the university the previous semester. Dr. Hannaford seemed to love his subject matter. When he lectured, he would walk back and forth at the front of the class, or up and down the aisles, keeping everyone's attention. Thanks to Dr. Hannaford's class, for the first time I understood and appreciated the creativity that's needed on the promotion side of marketing and its enormous influence in business and society.

The key to promotion is creativity. There is no one right way to promote a product. A method that's right for one product can be totally wrong for another. Or what worked to sell a product one year can be a failure the next.

The creative aspect of promotion suited my way of thinking and my background. It didn't take me long to realize that finally I had found my future profession and it was going to be marketing. I credit Dr. Hannaford, and the enthusiasm, passion, and excitement he brought to his promotion class, for my decision. After that class, I took a few more of his marketing classes and he became my academic advisor. Later, after graduation, he became a friend.

During the years 2002 to 2006, our second son, John, attended the University of Eau Claire and he also chose marketing as his major. Dr. Hannaford was John's academic advisor and his professor for several classes. I'm pleased that John went to the same university as his parents and selected marketing as his major, and I'm delighted he was a better student than his father.

My first professional job upon graduation was in computer sales. During my four years in this position, I visited and talked to many small business owners and learned about the computer industry and about small businesses. The computer or data processing industry was growing and changing rapidly. The personal computer had not been invented yet. At that time, the Burroughs small computer systems cost about fifty thousand dollars and required the space of a small room. Their processing power was smaller than the computing power available in any smart mobile phone of today.

In my discussions with small business owners, I always asked about their business history, how they started their businesses, and how they grew them over time. I found them to be regular people, like anyone else I knew, but they had the courage to take the risks involved in pursuing their own business ideas. The owners seemed pleased to share their stories—both their challenges and successes.

I started thinking that perhaps someday I would own my own business, but I couldn't imagine then what type of business I would start.

A year after we moved back to Eau Claire, in 1979, I enrolled at the university to pursue a master's degree in business, taking classes during evenings and Saturdays, while working full time.

In the last semester of my MBA program, I took an independent study class, supervised by Dr. Hannaford. International marketing had been one of my interests, and I decided to do a research project on export marketing practices by businesses in northwestern Wisconsin. During this semester-long project, I prepared a detailed questionnaire and sent it to eighty-five companies. Forty-one of them participated in the study. After I analyzed the responses, I wrote a sixty-seven-page paper about the objectives of the research, the methodology, and the findings. A summary of my study was published in the December 1982 issue of the *Wisconsin Business Journal*.

One of the major findings of my project was that export marketing represented a major opportunity for most small companies, but many businesses were not taking advantage of it. This new knowledge gave me the idea that export marketing was the ideal field for me to start my own business. It suited my international cultural background and my education, and it was a field of great interest to me. However, the time was not right. I needed more business experience and savings to use as start-up capital. I also needed to be living in a larger city with an international airport.

I completed the MBA program, with an emphasis in international marketing, in two years and graduated in December of 1981. The following year, after four years in computer sales, I was ready for something new. Shelley had been working for Wisconsin Telephone Company, an AT&T company, for three years by then, and through her I learned that AT&T was about to deregulate the telephone equipment side of its business and had established a new company, which was to be called AT&T Information Systems. I applied and was hired to work in Eau Claire, managing large accounts in northwestern Wisconsin.

My job was selling private branch exchange (PBX) telephone systems to hospitals, clinics, hotels, and other large companies. I did this successfully from 1982 to 1987, and then was promoted to national account manager and transferred to Minneapolis.

Throughout the first ten years of my business career in America, I hoped that I would find a way to return to Greece as an employee of an American company with operations in Greece. In the summer of 1988, I learned that AT&T International was growing its business in Greece and planned to appoint a new country manager there later that year. I applied for the position and was looking forward to an interview. I was thirty-four years old, had an MBA and six years of successful experience with AT&T with two promotions, was a native speaker of Greek and fluent in English.

While waiting to get a call for an interview, I read in an AT&T publication that a new country manager for Greece had already been appointed. He was sixty-one years old, and I later found out he did not speak Greek and had never been to Greece prior to his appointment.

After that, I decided there was no reason for me to stay with AT&T much longer. In the spring of 1989, the time was finally right to start my own company. I had more than ten years of experience in marketing and sales, we were living in Minneapolis, which has an international airport, and we had savings of about fifty thousand dollars we could use as starting capital.

I named our company World Trade Network, Ltd. The main idea was that we would find trading partners in several countries that would buy American products from us, and in turn we would buy their products to sell in the US.

Monday, April 3rd, 1989, was my first day of work as the president and only employee of World Trade Network, Ltd. I had converted the smallest bedroom in our house to an office with a large desk, personal computer and printer, fax machine, and separate business telephone line.

Our new business had an impressive sounding name with a professionally designed logo, no products to sell, and no clients or trading partners anywhere. Shelley was supportive. She was working for the regulated side of AT&T, managing customer service representatives. Her income was sufficient to cover our mortgage and living expenses.

We were willing to take the risk for a better lifestyle, more frequent and longer trips to Greece and to other places, and the freedom to run the business without office politics and unproductive meetings. We also hoped that our new business would be successful so that Shelley would be able to leave her job in a few years and come to work with me.

Around three o'clock in the afternoon of that first day, our two sons came home from school. Our oldest son, Bill, was eight years old and in second grade. He knew that it was his father's first day at work at his new company, and when he came home, he asked me, "How was your first day at work in your new company, Dad? Did you make a lot of money? I know you did!" That took me by surprise. I wasn't sure what to tell him, so I told him the truth.

"My day was good, Bill. I didn't make any money today, because it will take some time for our company to make money, but I had a good day. Our company will be making money later."

On that day, I wasn't sure when or how we would start making money, but I was optimistic. I didn't realize then that it would take us longer than 1 had expected, or that it would be so difficult.

These days, more than thirty years later, our family business is known as WTN Electronics, Ltd. It is owned and operated by our second son, John. It supplies marine electronics and spare parts to ship-owning companies and dealers that sell, install, and maintain marine electronics. We are a small company, but in the last thirty years we have developed an excellent reputation as a resourceful, responsive, and reliable business partner.

Our clients are in about forty countries around the world, with Greek customers contributing a large part of the company's annual revenue. Greece is the largest commercial-ship-owning country in the world. Greek shipowners own about 18% of the world's commercial ship capacity, so it makes sense that our company was started by a Greek. I wish I could say that starting the company was the result of my careful analysis and unique understanding of world market opportunities. But the reality is that it happened by coincidence and/or serendipity.

The weekend after I officially started my career as a business owner, I was shopping at the local mall with Shelley. In the center of the mall was a display of an electric catamaran-style boat. It was being displayed as a new product, and two men about my age were explaining its features and benefits. Mostly out of curiosity, I stopped to talk to them about their unusual product. I learned that it was the first product developed by their new company and they were looking for end users and distributors.

I explained my international background and my new business and asked if they planned to sell this new boat in the Mediterranean region. They agreed to give my company the exclusive sales rights for France, Italy, and Greece. They provided me with some leaflets and a price list, and now we had our first product to sell. I thought that since I would be traveling to Italy and Greece for other products, I could also try to find importers for this boat.

A week later, half a dozen of my former AT&T colleagues invited me to a celebratory goodbye lunch. During the lunch, one pointed out that I made a mistake leaving a good position with AT&T, that starting a small business was too risky. Another told me I looked more energized and happier than he had ever seen me and asked me what projects I was working on. I showed everyone a leaflet for the electric catamaran that I had in my pocket. Few of them thought it was a product worth pursuing. Some even laughed disparagingly. I didn't mind.

One of them said, "Ben, if you're going to be in the marine products business, you should go and talk to Stearns Company!"

I had never heard the words "Stearns Company" before, so I asked for more information. He explained that Stearns Manufacturing was the leading maker of life jackets and related items and was based in St. Cloud, Minnesota. I thanked him for his suggestion as our conversation moved on to other subjects. After I returned to my office that afternoon, I called the Stearns Company to see if there could be an opportunity for our cooperation. Indeed, there was.

The next day, I was in St. Cloud, an hour northwest of Minneapolis, visiting with the international sales manager of Stearns Company. By the end of our meeting, our new, small company was appointed the exclusive sales agent for Stearns products in France, Italy, and Greece, to be paid a 7.5% commission on sales.

One of the highlights of our discussion with Stearns was a special safety product known as a cold-water immersion suit, designed to be used by commercial ship crews. The suit is made of quarter inch-thick neoprene. It can keep afloat sailors forced to abandon ship in emergencies and keep them warm for at least twenty-four hours. I learned that most sailors who abandon ship do not die from drowning but from hypothermia, which can set in within minutes or up to four hours, depending on the water temperature. The international sea safety regulations known as Safety of Life at Sea (SOLAS) required that a number of these suits be mandatory on every commercial vessel effective July 1, 1991.

I returned to my office that day thinking that our young company was now in the marine safety market. A short time later we became sales agents for the same three countries in Europe for a company called ACR Electronics, which supplied products to Stearns.

We did not sell any of the electric catamaran boats. But, thanks to the connection I established with the men who developed it, and to my ex-AT&T colleague's suggestion to talk to Stearns, today our company is in the marine products business. Our successful cooperation with Stearns over our first ten years became the foundation of our business success.

In our first year, our total company revenue was less than $100,000 and did not cover our expenses. In the second year, our revenues were approximately $400,000 and we broke even. I did not pay myself a salary during those years. Success is almost never a sure thing in business. It certainly was not a sure thing in 1991 as we were starting our third year.

In the beginning of that year, I had high expectations because we had established several good clients and the first of July was the deadline for shipowners to purchase the required cold-water immersion suits that we and other companies were selling. I had been working long hours during the first two months, sending many offers, but by the end of February we had received only a few small orders. I was worried.

One evening in March, I finished my work at ten-thirty in the evening and then walked downstairs to our family room where Shelley had been watching the local evening news, sitting on a sofa with a blanket over her knees. She turned the television off as I sat on a leather La-Z-Boy chair. I closed my eyes and started rocking. I took a few deep breaths and the tension in my neck eased a bit.

Shelley must have noticed my tiredness but didn't say anything for a minute or two. When I opened my eyes and looked at her, she said, "You look tired. How was your work today?"

I said, "It was a long day, but I'm not sure how it went. I sent a lot of offers but we're not getting orders." My voice was breaking as if I were about to cry, something I hadn't done since I was a child.

I don't know if that was a moment of weakness or strength, but I felt the need to share my doubts about the success of our business. I stared at the dark television and continued, "The last two months were not good, and I'm not sure how the rest of the year will go. This is a critical year for the business. The fifty-thousand dollars of our capital is gone, and I had no salary for two years. We need more sales, but I don't know what else to do." I finally found the courage to look at her.

Shelley looked back at me thoughtfully and didn't say anything right away. She looked tired, as this was her usual bedtime and she had been up since six. Then she asked, "Do you think you're doing the things that are needed for the success of the business?"

Her question surprised me and impressed me with its wisdom, as did the calm and confident tone of her delivery. I had not thought about that before. I took a few moments to mentally review my recent marketing and sales activities. Had I sent enough offers to customers, in the most professional manner I could? Was I missing something?

I couldn't think of anything else I could be doing. I looked at her and said, "Yes, I think I've been doing the right things, but I'm not sure if we'll get the orders we need to have a good year."

Shelley's immediate response, again in a confident voice, was "If you're doing the right things and you keep doing them, the orders will come. There's plenty of time left in the year. I see no reason to worry."

What a rational business analysis this was and a confidence booster for me! Suddenly, things looked better. I recovered my usual voice, stood up from my chair, smiled at Shelley, walked over and, as she also stood up, I hugged and kissed her. We were both smiling. That moment was a key turning point in my attitude and confidence. The next day I continued to do what I thought were the right things for the success of our business.

At the end of that year our revenues were about $750,000, and we had a net profit of $150,000 before I paid myself a salary. We had recovered our initial capital investment and were a profitable company. We had clients in several countries, with several product lines in the marine and other areas, and on our way to success.

In 1992, we used part of the previous year's profit to build an addition to our house, of approximately 1,200 square feet, to be our business office, with its own entrance, an employee restroom, and a small kitchen area, and we hired our first employee. Two years later, in 1994, the company was doing well enough that we no longer needed the security of Shelley's AT&T position and salary.

Shelley joined our company as vice president, and we hired another assistant. Shelley designed and implemented automated systems for our billing and our accounts receivable and payable that made our daily operations more efficient and effective and have been instrumental to our success.

I've been fortunate to work with clients in about forty countries and to visit thirty of them. I've learned that one commodity that's in short supply in business and especially in international business is trust. One must earn trust through personal and professional communications and actions. I learned from my mother that any trade must be beneficial to both parties, and to look your trading partners in the eye and make sure they know your life story and how you work, and to always deliver more than you promise.

Normally we would start to communicate with new international clients via mail or fax. Later I would try to visit them in their office at the earliest opportunity. I noticed that our business relationships with clients I had met in person were always better than with the clients I had not met. Many clients have told me that they liked working with our company better than other American companies, they worked with, because they knew my immigration story and felt that our company was sensitive and respectful of their own culture and other differences.

Often their English communication was incorrect or incomplete, but I understood them anyway because I had made similar language mistakes. I knew what they meant, handled their requests promptly and with attention to details.

Many businesspeople talk often about their goal of delivering superior customer service. In my experience, few businesspeople understand that "superior customer service" is most often delivered through "superior communications." I've made superior communication the foundation of my business philosophy and, I believe, it has been the main reason for our business success. Many of our clients have told me that our communications to them, via fax or later via email, were the most clear, easy to understand, and complete of all the messages they had received from all their suppliers.

I've learned that each country has its own culture and approach to business. In Europe, I found the Dutch easy to work with and good international businesspeople. The Italians are just as good or better, but a lot more hospitable and friendly. The same is true of the businesspeople I have worked with in Greece and Turkey. I found the French more difficult, the British less reliable than most Europeans, and the Germans efficient but less imaginative.

I have worked with Chinese and Japanese clients and suppliers and have visited these countries for business, for one week each. In China, I spent half the week in Beijing and the other half in Shanghai. I found the Chinese to be reliable and responsive. I was impressed with the Great Wall, which I visited with a local guide named Naixiang Feng. Naixiang had worked in our company for a few months as an intern while he was working on his master's degree in business at St. Thomas University in Minneapolis.

I found Shanghai, with its futuristic ambiance, the most progressive city of any that I've seen. That impression hasn't changed, even though it's been twenty years since I was there. Based on what I saw in China and my experience working with a few Chinese companies, I became convinced that China would surpass the United States in the size of its economy and its dominance of world trade a lot sooner than most people expected.

Japan seemed to me to be more focused on its past rather than the future. I found the conformist attitude and lack of imagination of its culture to be obstacles in international business, even though I've met and worked with several progressive and effective Japanese international businesspeople.

Istanbul, Turkey, was another city I enjoyed visiting. By 1998, I made half a dozen business trips to Istanbul and established several steady clients and some friends there. From many parts of this City of Seven Hills you can see parts of the twenty-mile-long stretch of the Bosporus Strait, which divides the city in two, and Europe from Asia. Its width ranges from half a mile to two miles and is one of Istanbul's most beguiling sights.

While crossing the Bosporus by boat in 1998, I had an unusual and unforgettable experience. I usually took these boats from the European side, where I stayed, to visit clients on the Asian side. A taxi took me to the nearest boat station, then after taking a boat across the strait I would hail another taxi on the other side. I found that taking these boats was the most pleasant and scenic way to get across the strait. The ticket price is about one dollar each way, and boats depart every five or ten minutes from various well-marked departure points along the business districts. Typical transit time from one side to the other is about ten minutes depending on traffic and the departure station. Most boats are double-deckers, the size of a bus, and open on all sides, with good visibility.

About four-thirty in the afternoon on a pleasantly warm November day with a cool sea breeze, I took a taxi on the Asian side, to the nearest boat station to return to my hotel after finishing my client meetings.

As I boarded the small double-decker boat, I was reviewing my day in my head. The prospective clients I met had been friendly and hospitable, and the prospects for good business cooperation seemed bright. I was forty-four years old and in excellent health, and our ten-year-old company was successful and growing. I loved my job, traveling to cities like Istanbul, and working with clients who were professional, independent small-business owners.

Boarding the boat, I saw a handful of passengers sitting on the lower level. I walked to the upper level for a better view and had the whole deck to myself. I was standing, leaning against the back of the wooden bench in front of me for support. I set my leather briefcase on the bench and looked around the strait in all directions. To the southwest, I recognized the minarets of the Hagia Sophia and the Blue Mosque from my previous visits. The sun was setting, painting the sky, behind the minarets, gold orange, and spotlighting the long, skinny clouds in the background. It was a serene and romantic sunset, the type that tugs at your heartstrings and you can feel inside you.

I was relaxed and breathed the cool sea air with satisfaction. The views around me were even more beautiful than usual, bathed in the golden glow of the sunset. The dark blue of the sea and its calmness were interrupted by small waves pulsing with a tinge of sunset gold. Several other passenger boats were leisurely crossing the strait in both directions, leaving behind white water trails. Further south, the outlines of larger ships waiting for permission to enter the strait were silhouetted against the sky.

Suddenly, the public address systems from several mosques in the city began, one after another, broadcasting the Islamic calls to prayer. I had experienced these calls many times in my previous visits to Istanbul and I usually found them exotic and melodious. This time their effect was totally different.

As I stood on the upper deck all alone, in the middle of the Bosporus, surrounded by the gold pulsing sea and watching the dreamy sunset, the sudden, hypnotic calls to prayer transported me to a new and delightful dimension.

Time seemed to slow, as did my breathing. My senses became the most acute I could remember. Everything around me appeared brighter and sharper. I saw myself from above, standing on a boat in the middle of the strait that separates Europe and Asia. Then, I was overwhelmed with a euphoric feeling and the sensation that I was in the center of the world and one with the universe. I felt I belonged there; I was meant to be in that beautiful scene, and it was part of the purpose of my life.

Everything was in just the right spot at just the right time! I was experiencing a celestial symphony of colors, sights, and sounds, all arranged for me in a perfect combination. Being in the center of it all, I was overcome with incredible joy and happiness.

I had an urge to share this intense and marvelous experience with someone. I looked around but I was still alone on the upper deck. I reached in my pocket for my Motorola flip phone and called our office in Minnesota to speak to my wife and business partner, Shelley. It was about nine o´clock in the morning in Minnesota when Shelley answered.

I said, "Shelley, you will not believe this! I am having the most amazing experience of my life. I am on a passenger boat in the middle of the Bosporus, and I feel like I am at the center of the universe!"

"That's wonderful, Ben!" Shelley said, laughing, and added, "You haven't been drinking, have you?"

"No, I have not been drinking. I had good client meetings this afternoon and now I'm returning to the European side, to my hotel. You would not believe the views. The sun is setting, and it is beautiful all around me. I feel a cool breeze on my face, and I hear the calls to prayer from the mosques all around the city. It's a wonderful feeling, like an intense spiritual experience."

Shelley tried to be supportive as usual. "That sounds great, Ben. I'm happy for you. It must be quite a sight. You'll have to take me there someday."

"Yes," I said, "we will come here together, someday. I'll tell you more about this when I get to the hotel," and ended my call.

I stood there in amazement, looking intensely around me, trying to capture it, to imprint everything to my memory. I was still feeling elated and joyful, hoping these feelings would stay with me.

Soon afterward, the calls to prayer began to slow and fade away. My breathing became normal again. Time resumed its regular rhythm and I noticed that my boat was approaching the passenger terminal. I scanned the horizon all around the boat one more time. Everything seemed normal, but I was in a euphoric mood as I left the boat and walked toward the taxi area.

It has now been more than twenty years since that amazing Istanbul experience. I've often tried to understand the nature of that unforgettable event in my life. Did I experience what is known in Buddhism as nirvana—a state of perfect happiness? Is this something we should strive to achieve in our lives?

I do not have answers to these questions. What I do know is that many people, at some point in their lives, have moments of a heightened state of awareness that last a limited time and produce a sense of euphoria and peace. Perhaps these experiences are meant to show us our unity with the universe, to help us appreciate our place in it and to draw inspiration, peace, and strength.

For those few, precious moments on the Bosporus, all my senses and my entire being seemed to be in perfect alignment with the world and the universe. That experience has helped me to appreciate the many blessings of my life, my choices, and opportunities, and I will always be grateful for that.

Ten years later, I kept my promise to Shelley, and we visited Istanbul together, on a cruise. We enjoyed our twenty-four hours we spent in the city and the views from the ship, in our approach and departure. It was a pleasant tourist experience and not the kind I had earlier.

Three Trips to America

WHEN MY PARENTS, VASSILIS AND Maria, started their lives in the 1920s, almost a century ago, in the small village of Krania on Mount Olympus, the world was a different place. They had received only a sixth-grade education, which I think served them well. When they became parents one of their highest priorities in life was to see their children well educated.

Vassilis started working at thirteen, as an apprentice carpenter in the village. Maria at thirteen was helping with work in the family fields and assisting her mother with household chores like cooking and cleaning and making cheese from the milk of their herd of goats. After Vassilis and Maria were married they continued to work hard to raise their family and were able to navigate well the world of their time.

In the early 1940s, because of the German occupation, they were forced to become war refugees for over a year and had to live in army barracks in Larissa. In the late 1940s, Vassilis served three years in the Greek army fighting during the civil war.

When they joined their lives in marriage, in December of 1951, life in the village had started to slowly return to a semblance of normalcy. Everyone there was poor, but this did not seem to worry Vassilis and Maria. They were young and they formed a union of one mind in their strong work ethic, in frugality, and in how they chose to raise their family. They depended on and trusted each other and were confident in their abilities as a strong team.

In Homer's *Odyssey*, Odysseus, having his wife, Penelope, in mind, says to Princess Nausicaä, "There is nothing more admirable than when two people who see eye to eye, keep house as man and wife, confounding their enemies and delighting their friends."

These words capture how my parents have spent their forty-seven years together as husband and wife. My father was an introvert and dignified man of few words who minded his own business. When he went to the coffee shop and happened to be sitting with gossipers, he would move to another table. His favorite pastimes were playing backgammon with his friends at the coffee shop, reading the daily newspaper, and listening to the radio. When we moved to the city, he purchased a portable transistor radio for our home. He knew that he and his entire family would enjoy the music and he was right.

When he started to buy an Athens newspaper on his way home from work every day, he didn't realize how it would expand my view of the world. He was pleased when he saw my brother and me read it. I dare say that this daily national newspaper was one of the most important gifts I ever received from my father because it enabled me to start broadening my horizons at the age of ten. The new world horizons blossomed into a global awareness that has been invaluable my whole life. I suspect that without that early, daily exposure to national news and international stories, my life would not be as rich.

My father was a master carpenter and construction worker. He worked with concrete forms, could lay bricks, do stucco work, and anything else relating to construction. He built our house in Larissa practically by himself, working evenings and weekends, after his regular job.

He worked for only a few contractors his whole career because his bosses appreciated his workmanship and dependability. He never missed a day of work, he arrived early and left late, and he delivered a full day's work for his wages. He liked his work, but he had higher aspirations for his two sons. He often told us that construction work was difficult because it is mostly manual labor, and one is always exposed to the weather—the extreme heat of Greek summers and the cold and rain of the winters. He told us often that his major goal in life was that he would not see us become construction workers. He wanted us to get a good education and professions that would utilize our minds rather than our muscles.

Fortunately, we did not disappoint him. My brother and I worked several summers in construction and got a taste of it, but we ended up with careers in an office environment "working with our minds and with clean hands," as my father would say. He was satisfied and proud of that.

I am proud of my father and the success he had in life. He honored his parents and helped them have a decent retirement and comfortable old age, and he helped his sister and her family, when she became a widow at a fairly young age and never remarried. He was a beloved husband, father of three, and grandfather of seven.

My mother, Maria, had almost the opposite personality as my father. She was an extrovert who loved to talk. She was quick with a greeting, a smile, and a pleasant word for everyone she met. She was frugal in her spending but generous with her hospitality and friendliness. When we lived in our village, she knew everyone. If a visitor from another village happened to walk by the road outside our house, she would invite the stranger in our yard for a glass of water or a coffee, a piece of fruit or whatever we had available. Her sharp memory enabled her to remember faces and names, and up to her old age she still recalled a dozen or more telephone numbers of her relatives and friends.

She was so articulate and so quick with just the right response in discussions that her brother, Giorgos, called her "the district attorney." She would probably have made a great lawyer if she had been educated. She thought that "the district attorney" suited her. She was pleased and proud when our first son, Bill, was accepted into law school and became an attorney.

Other than taking care of her family, her two favorite activities were gardening and doing needlepoint lace work. Her love of flowers become legend in our village for two reasons. First, she would share her flowers from our village yard with anyone who admired them. And she always remembered to give those admirers a cutting at the right season so they could grow their own. To this day, when I walk around the village, I often see rosebushes and other plants in bloom that owe their roots to cuttings supplied by my mother.

On her first trip to America, she brought with her a live basil plant. When the agricultural customs officer found it in her large handbag and confiscated it, my mother made such a big fuss, in Greek, that someone had to come and fetch me from the waiting area to go inside and explain to my mother why she was not allowed to bring a live plant into the US.

While she was visiting us in Minnesota, she loved the yellow evening primroses in our yard and was delighted to hear that the USA had no law about taking live plants outside of the country. Soon afterwards, almost our entire village had this "new American yellow flower" in the yards. Over the years, our yard design in our village home changed, and we lost the yellow evening primroses. But every June, as we walk around our Greek village, we see the intense yellow primroses in other gardens and I immediately see in my mind my mother's face smiling as if to say, *See? I am gone but my American primroses are still here.* They are indeed, and so is my mother, in many people's memories and in my mind and my heart!

In the 1980s, after my father retired, I brought my parents to the US to stay with us for a three-month period in 1982, in 1984, and in 1988. On their first trip they flew from Athens to Chicago, and Shelley and I and our five-month-old son were waiting for them at O'Hare Airport.

My mother was emotional about being in Chicago, where her father had spent some time about seventy years earlier. We took a drive in the Greek town and other ethnic neighborhoods where Greek immigrants of the early 1990s may have lived as we had no records of any address from my grandfather's time in Chicago. My mother kept saying, "Maybe this is a street that your grandfather walked as a young man." She was moved and pleased that she was in Chicago, being driven around in a large comfortable car by her son, Evangelos, the grandson of the uneducated Evangelos Matos who came as a young immigrant to America seventy-three years earlier.

I asked my mother what she thought her father would think if he could see her now, being driven around Chicago. She said she didn't think that he would have believed it, as she found it difficult herself to comprehend being in Chicago, in America.

In 1982, I was twenty-eight years old. I was married to an American wife and had a son. I was also a graduate of an American university with two degrees. I was working in a management position with AT&T, the largest corporation in America then, with about 350,000 employees. I thought about how fortunate I was that I grew up in a different time. Even though I was also an immigrant, my life and my immigration experience had been a lot easier than my grandfather's. My knowledge of English, the available means of transportation to get here, the job opportunities and living conditions all contributed to a smoother, comfortable transition for me and my generation and to a better life.

Some of the questions I had while driving in Chicago with my parents—and are still on my mind many years later—are if my grandfather had not been an immigrant to America, would I be in America today? How much of my thinking had been affected by having a grandfather who had spent his young adult life in America? Was my coming to America embedded in my genes by inheriting my grandfather's personality? Or had the stories I heard as a child, from my mother about her father's life influenced my choices? I still don't have answers to these questions.

I did not bring up these questions to discuss with my parents. At that time and for many years afterward, my parents were hoping I would decide to leave America and return with my wife and children to live in Greece. For at least the first ten years of my life in America, I too, was keeping that option open.

In 1988, my parents came to spend three months with us for the third and last time. We visited the city of Duluth, Minnesota, where my grandfather had also spent some time. My mother had a similar experience being driven around in Duluth that she had had six years earlier in Chicago. She felt that she was reconnecting with her father who had been dead for almost twenty years.

In 1988, I was thirty-four years old and about to start my own business. My parents knew that the probability that I would return to live in Greece was not high, but they were not disappointed. They were happy to see me living a comfortable life with my wife and children, in a nice home, neighborhood, and city.

Most of all, my parents were delighted that I did marry Shelley, an American wife! In their three visits to America, they had plenty of opportunities to get to know Shelley's personality and to appreciate her skills and talents as a wife and mother. They loved their "American daughter." My mother never tired of telling me, at least a few times each week, how glad she was that I did not follow her advice and that I had married Shelley. She was convinced that there was no other woman, in Greece, in America or any other country, who would have made a better wife and mother than Shelley. This was music to my ears.

As a parent myself, I have made my share of mistakes in trying to figure out what was better or best for our two sons. I was fortunate to learn from my mother's generous admission that her advice to me not to marry an American was wrong, and I tried to remember that. I recognized that as a father, I did not have all the information about what was best for our two sons, especially after they completed their university education and became responsible and self-sufficient adults. I am glad to see them satisfied with their chosen professions and happy in their lives.

TWENTY-SEVEN

Two Countries to Call Home

Staying as I am, one foot in one country and the other in another, I find my condition to be very happy.

Rene Descartes

THERE ARE ABOUT FORTY-FIVE MILLION people living in the United States today who were born in another country. That's nearly fourteen percent of the population. Why do people choose to make their home in another country? I imagine there are many reasons, but probably the most common one is for a better life. Some change countries by necessity as war refugees, or as immigrants looking for work, and some were brought to America as children.

French philosopher Rene Descartes, the father of modern Western philosophy, was probably one of few of his era who decided to live in a country other than that of his birth. He was born to a wealthy family in France, in 1596, and when he was twenty-two, he went to the Netherlands as a student. Later he returned to live in Amsterdam for more than twenty of his fifty-four years of life. He said that in the Netherlands he was able to enjoy great liberty not found elsewhere, and that it was quieter and more suitable to his lifestyle and his work. He was also able to take frequent trips to France and other places.

The imagery of his quote—straddling two worlds, with one foot in France and one in the Netherlands—helped me to understand and appreciate my lifelong search for a place to call home, which, like Descartes, turned out to be two countries instead of one.

In August of 1964, when I was ten, we were getting ready to move from my first home, our village on Mount Olympus, to Larissa, a city about twenty miles away. During the last month before our move, my maternal grandmother, Katerina, whom we saw every day, kept telling us she was sad that we were moving to what she called the "foreign lands." The Greek word she used for foreign lands was *Xenetia*, which comes from *Xenos*, meaning foreigner. This is also the root word for xenophobia, the fear of anything foreign.

I was surprised to hear Grandma say that we were going to "foreign lands," because I knew that Larissa was not far, and it was a Greek city. I asked my mother, "Why is Yiayia saying we're going to Xenetia and why is she crying and looking sad all the time? We're not going to Xenetia, we are going to Larissa."

My mother said, "Don't mind your Yiayia. To her, anyplace outside our village is Xenetia. She is sad because she is used to seeing you every day and she will miss you when we're in Larissa."

I accepted my mother's answer, but I wasn't sure I understood Yiayia's point. I started to wonder if we were leaving our village home forever.

I knew that our paternal grandparents were staying in our village, and I assumed that our house there would continue to be our home but, in addition to that, we would have another home in Larissa, and I liked that.

After we moved to the city, I liked all the conveniences of our new home and the educational and entertainment options the city offered. I decided our new home was better than our old one, and, for the next seven years, Larissa was my true home. Our village home was simply where I was born and lived during my childhood and where we spent the summer months. I did not realize then how deeply rooted in my soul our village home was, and how significant it would become later in my life.

When I first came to America, in 1971, as a foreign exchange student, I knew that I was a visitor and a guest, and my real home was in

Greece, where I expected to return and spend the rest of my life.

For the first time in my life, during that year in Barron, I experienced missing my family and my home. What exactly was I missing? I figured that what I missed was a mixture that included good times with my immediate family, my mother's cooking, my brother's jokes, the warm climate, and the fun times with my friends in our favorite hangouts.

When I returned to Greece in 1972 and readjusted to Greek life, I realized that my view of the world had changed. My year in Wisconsin gave me the confidence to believe that even though my home was in Larissa, Greece, it could also be in America. This made it easier for me to return to America in 1974, to attend the university at Eau Claire. Living there for four years as a student, I became more comfortable with the American way of life.

My university academic advisor, Dr. Hannaford, whom I had asked to write a letter of recommendation to Burroughs Corporation, where I got my first professional job, told me that in his letter he wrote, "Ben is as American as baseball and apple pie."

At first, I was not sure how to take this, because I always considered myself Greek, but since the letter helped me get the job, I didn't mind. I figured, when in America do as Americans do, but I would continue to be Greek.

The longer I stayed in America, the more I realized that it offered special benefits and opportunities for a better life. In 1978, as I was getting ready to marry Shelley, I delayed my return to Greece for a few years, because of better career opportunities. I also did not want to serve twenty-four months in the Greek army, which was mandatory for Greek males.

The few years we were planning to stay in Eau Claire soon became more than ten, and our two sons were born there. Eau Claire became another home for me, and the only home our sons knew for their first few years.

Later, when I thought about moving back to Greece, even though Shelley was ready to move there, our sons' future educational and career opportunities, and their future obligation to serve in the Greek army, became important variables in our calculations. These variables did not factor in favor of Greece as our permanent home, and our return there was further delayed.

In 1987, our family moved to a suburb of Minneapolis. Shelley and I were promoted to better positions with more responsibilities and better pay, and we felt that it would be better for us and our children to live in a large metropolitan area like Minneapolis-St. Paul. We have been living there for thirty-four years, much longer than any other place.

Why did we stay in Minnesota for so long and not return to Greece to live, as was my original plan and as I had promised my parents?

After my marriage to Shelley and the complete acceptance of her by my family, I realized that my mother's admonition, "Don't marry an American," was not about a future American wife. What she meant was, "Don't stay in America."

I understood then that my mother was influenced by the choice her father had made when he returned from America in 1925, after his sixteen years' stay as an immigrant. He chose to stay in Greece, rather than return to America, and he had a good and happy life.

My mother assumed that my returning to live in Greece was going to be the best choice for me, like it was for her father fifty years earlier. Her assumption would be reasonable if the world had stayed the same. But the world changed, as it always does.

My mother could not foresee that, in her lifetime, her son would live in America and be able to visit his family in Greece twice each year. Or that he would speak with her on the phone from America practically every day, and that she and her husband would visit America three times in her lifetime.

It's clear to me now that her implied admonition, "Don't stay in America," was not different from her mother's thinking, that any place outside her own small village was a foreign land. As the years went by, life surprised my mother and me in unexpected and delightful ways.

Starting in 1984, Shelley and I with our two sons visited Greece every other year for about four weeks, so my parents got to know their "American grandchildren" as they were growing up.

Five years later, I began to visit Greece in the spring and fall of every year for the needs of my own business. During these visits, I visited our clients in Athens and spent a long weekend with my parents and the rest of my family. At first, my family could not believe they were seeing me every six months. We often joked that if I were living in Athens, perhaps they would see me only once a year.

When I started my own international business, one of my goals was to be able to spend more time in Greece. Shelley and I wanted to take advantage of the best of what Greece has to offer: good times with family and friends, wonderful weather, the special swimming joy of the Aegean Sea, the unparalleled beauty of the Greek islands, tasty fruits and vegetables, reliving my happy childhood memories in our village, and much more. We also wanted to enjoy the best that America has to offer: good times with family and friends, better educational and career opportunities for ourselves and our children and grandchildren, comfortable working conditions and lifestyle, and much more.

We've been fortunate to have one home in Greece and one in America, and to enjoy both. That choice has been a particularly good one for Shelley and me, for our sons, and for our extended families.

By the time my parents started visiting us, America was no longer Xenetia for them, but another family home, filled with their children and grandchildren, with love, comfort, and security, and with Greek food, wine, and music.

After my parents died, Shelley and I became the owners of the family house in Krania, in 2007, and renovated it with all modern conveniences, including a reliable internet connection and a digital piano for Shelley.

I had promised Shelley a piano a few years before, and when I purchased a portable Yamaha model, she was surprised and delighted. She was able to continue to play without missing her piano in Minnesota. We had not realized how important the piano would become in Shelley's embrace of our new summer home and of the Greek culture.

Because she has more free time to play in Greece, she used her knowledge of software and the digital capabilities of the piano to create her own arrangements and scores of her favorite Greek songs. She also learned the Greek lyrics, as part of her ongoing efforts to become fluent in Greek. Now she plays and sings, in Greek, a repertoire of about forty songs of various Greek composers, including the well-known Manos Hatzidakis and Mikis Theodorakis.

During the summer, we host music evenings on our patio, where Shelley's piano playing and singing is the entertainment. This has been a source of great fun for Shelley, because even though she does not like performing in front of public audiences, she loves to share her music with family and friends. It has also been a wonderful way to share her appreciation of Greek culture via the international language of music, and to make the Greek house of my birth her own beloved summer home.

My grandfather's sweet violin music, which went away more than sixty years earlier, has finally returned in the form of beautiful piano music to fill the house, the patio, and the yard of the violin player. My grandfather, Yiannis, would be so pleased and proud to know that live music has returned home, and that his grandson who left as a ten-year-old boy has also returned, as an adult, to his first home he loved as a young boy, to spend his summers there. These circles of life are now complete.

Having internet access enabled us to run our business from the house, so in 2007 we started spending the summer months in Krania. I often wonder what my maternal grandfather, Evangelos, who immigrated to America for work, would think of his grandson "working in America" from his house in the Greek village. No one could have predicted that.

The small, six-by-four-foot wooden balcony of our village home is now made of concrete and is eighteen feet long and seven feet wide but has the same spectacular views. We have kept our mother's tradition of beautiful red geraniums in the yard. We enjoy them together with plentiful aromatic basil and the beauty and aroma of the rosebushes she planted, and the red-orange blossoms of two pomegranate trees I have planted.

Shelley and I appreciate our daily walks in the trails above the village with stunning views of the valley below, and we enjoy our frequent visits to several nearby beaches of the clean and beautiful Aegean Sea.

Shelley and Ben Kyriagis, pencil drawing by Christina Papaioannou, in 2018.

In late July and early August, I enjoy picking oregano that grows wild on the hillsides above our village. I dry it in the shade for a couple weeks and then press it through a colander like special container, made by my father, to keep only the dried flowers and small leaves, which I pack in small glass jars to give away to family and friends. The pungent aroma of this oregano can only be described as how oregano was meant to smell.

Perhaps most of all, I enjoy living in our Krania home and walking in our village because the people there and every street and corner help bring back many wonderful childhood memories.

Now in my mid-sixties, I hope that Rene Descartes would not mind me changing his words slightly. Staying as I am, one foot in America and the other in Greece, I find my condition to be happy.

Stories and Compassion

I BELIEVE THAT LIFE IS A precious gift. We do not earn it, but we earn our life story through our choices, our words, and our actions. The stories we hear in our youth, and the stories we create and tell in our lives, make us who we become, as we navigate and celebrate our journey into the grand ocean of human history.

As the late writer Barry Lopez has said so eloquently, "All that is holding us together [are] stories and compassion." Compassion for ourselves, and everyone that we meet along our way. Stories and compassion evoke the emotions that connect us with our inner selves, with people near and far, with knowledge and truth and with the grandeur and meaning of our shared humanity.

I am optimistic by nature and I believe that humanity progresses, even though at times the progress seems to move slowly. I have learned that knowledge comes in small nuggets, and if we are not vigilant, we miss them. I hope that the world will continue to produce stories that offer new knowledge and compassion, which, in turn, will enable more people to breathe easier, with justice and better opportunities, on a well-cared-for planet.

My life has helped me to realize that we usually do not know if it will be our first, second, or even third choices that will make our lives better. Perhaps, as the late poet Mary Oliver has said, we need to keep "some room in our hearts for the unimaginable," and the unexpected.

I'm sharing my family's stories to honor and thank my parents, grandparents, and other teachers for everything they have taught me. Perhaps these stories can inspire others to share their own, as part of their legacy, and the documented record of our shared humanity.

We have instilled in our sons the desire to get a university education and to select a field of study and a profession that suited their interests and talents. I hope that our grandchildren, Ben, Max, and Ellen will be well served by this approach and by these sentiments:

From a Unitarian blessing: "Be kind in all you do. Search for what is true. Build a fair and peaceful world and care for the Earth and all who call her home."

From Judge Charles D. Gill: "There are many wonderful things that will never be done, if you do not do them."

Finally, Ben, Max, and Ellen, do marry an American! A Greek, a Canadian, or whomever you fall in love with. And do create and share your own life stories and pass them on to your children and grandchildren.

I dedicate this book to our children and grandchildren, to the memory of my parents and grandparents, and to my American wife of forty-three years, Shelley, who has been my greatest fortune and continues to fill my life's journey with joy.

* THE END *